Wiltshire
MURDERS

Nicola Sly

The History Press

ALSO BY THE AUTHOR

Bristol Murders
Cornish Murders (with John Van der Kiste)
Dorset Murders
Hampshire Murders
Somerset Murders (with John Van der Kiste)

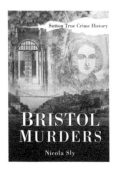
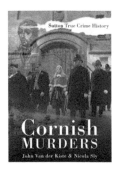
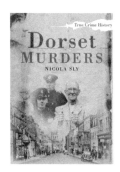

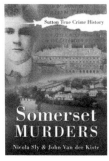
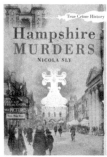

First published 2009

Reprinted 2011

The History Press
The Mill, Brimscombe Port
Stroud, Gloucestershire, GL5 2QG
www.thehistorypress.co.uk

British Library Cataloguing in Publication Data.
A catalogue record for this book is available from the British Library.

ISBN 978 0 7524 4896 1

Typesetting and origination by The History Press
Printed in Great Britain

CONTENTS

Author's Note & Acknowledgements   5

1. 'Nothing but skin and bone'   7
   Bradford-on-Avon, 1811

2. 'God bless you all!'   9
   Purton Stoke, 1819

3. 'May I be damned to everlasting if I had anything to do   14
   with the hatchet'
   Sutton Benger, 1820

4. 'I did it in a passion, seeing my wife and children ill-used'   19
   Littleton Drew, 1828

5. 'Thee will be hanged if thee hast a hundred necks'   22
   Lacock, 1828

6. 'You may as well let me poison it'   25
   Warminster, 1830

7. 'Oh, my God! I am a ruined woman!'   29
   Highworth, 1835

8. 'Damn your eyes, get up, or I'll kill you directly'   33
   Box, 1841

9. 'They say I murdered my baby?'   37
   Westbury, 1849

10. 'Beat the old bastard's brains out!'   43
    Trowbridge, 1854

11. 'Pardon me'   46
    Tollard Royal, 1859

12. 'I have done it. You had better lock me up'   50
    Devizes, 1881

13. 'I intended no harm to my old father'   53
    Lower Westbrook, 1885

14. 'What was the dispute as to the child about?'   59
    Devizes, 1889

15. 'Do you want me, Sir?'   64
    Melksham, 1892

16. 'The curse of my life'   68
    Swindon, 1903

17. 'I have told you the truth. He is where I have taken him to'   72
    Burbage, 1907

18. 'Stop that man; he has murdered my Teddy'   77
    Salisbury, 1908

19. 'I will make this county ring!'   84
    Enford, 1913

20. 'Diagnosis: alcoholism'   88
    Sutton Veny, 1917

21. 'I done the job and am prepared to stand the consequences'   93
    Long Newnton, 1924

22. 'You have got me, you rotter'   97
    Trowbridge, 1925

23. 'I'll see she shan't live to have the laugh over me'   103
    Durrington, 1939

24. 'Either you do what I want you to do or you die'   110
    Marlborough, 1943

25. 'She made Chris go away'   115
    Swindon, 1953

26. 'Everyone said she was too perfect to live'   119
    Salisbury, 1953

    Bibliography & References   124

    Index   125

AUTHOR'S NOTE & ACKNOWLEDGEMENTS

Wiltshire is a county that is steeped in history. It is famed for its ancient monuments such as Stonehenge and the Avebury Stone Circle, as well as the white horses carved into its chalky hillsides. Yet that history also includes numerous murders and one of England's earliest serial killers.

When Rebecca Smith was charged with the murder of her baby son, Richard, in 1849, she pleaded not guilty. However, when the jury at her trial found otherwise, she confessed before her execution to having poisoned seven more of her children for no better reason than that she was afraid that they would 'come to want'.

Thus Mrs Smith joins a diverse collection of child killers, spurned and jealous lovers, and those who murdered for greed or revenge. In 1819, Robert Watkins killed in the course of a highway robbery and, two years later, Edward Buckland killed an elderly widow simply because she would not let him into her cottage to warm himself by the fire. Wanting a place by the fire was also the motive for a murder in Devizes workhouse in 1881, while Swindon woman Mrs Court met her death in 1953 because one of her lodgers believed that the food she served was 'the worst he had ever eaten'.

As usual, I have numerous people to thank for their assistance and encouragement in compiling this collection. Roger Evans and John J. Eddleston have previously published books, the former on mystery and murder in Wiltshire, the latter a more general reference works on British murders and executions. These books are recorded in more detail in the bibliography, as are the local and national newspapers, which proved an invaluable source of material. Kay Taylor's article for the *Wiltshire Archaeological and Natural History Magazine* provided a fascinating insight into the Sutton Benger murder of 1820. John Broderick helped to source some of the photographs, including the one of victim Esther Swinford. My thanks must also go to the staff of the Central Library in Swindon and the Wiltshire and Swindon History Centre in Chippenham for their help in my research.

I must also thank John Van der Kiste for his sage advice and of course my husband, Richard, who, as always, helped with the proof reading and photography, and acted as chauffeur for a whistle-stop tour around Wiltshire, during which most of the photographs for the book were taken. Both he and my father, John Higginson, have supported me from the first word of this book to the last.

Finally, my thanks must go to my editor at The History Press, Matilda Richards, for her continued help and encouragement.

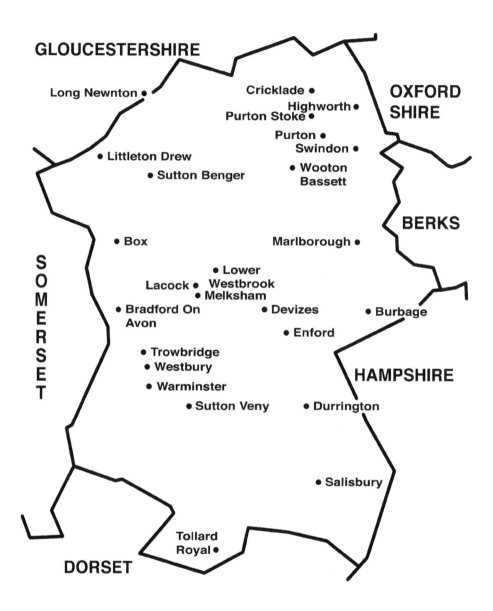

Map of Wiltshire.

1

'NOTHING BUT SKIN AND BONE'

Bradford-on-Avon, 1811

Samuel Tucker of Bradford-on-Avon had originally worked as a weaver, but by 1811 he had been practising medicine and calling himself Dr Tucker for some time.

Samuel was married to Ann, a widow with children, who was twenty-five years his senior. It is not known whether he simply tired of living with his wife or whether he found another, possibly younger, woman, but at the end of 1810 Samuel Tucker devised a fiendish plan to rid himself of Ann forever, while making it seem as though she had actually died from natural causes.

From New Year's Day 1811, Tucker kept Ann confined to her bedroom. She was not allowed to receive any visitors and was fed only occasionally by her husband on small quantities of half-boiled potatoes, barley bread and sips of water. Tucker intended not to starve Ann to death but to keep her alive, although in such a severely weakened condition that she would fall prey to the slightest illness.

Several times, Tucker's work took him away from home for a couple of days. Whenever that happened, he would simply lock the door and windows of his wife's bedroom, forcing her to lie in her own urine and excrement, in the closed, airless room. A broadsheet published at the time described the atmosphere in the room as 'nearly sufficient to create putridity'.

Ann slowly became weaker and more emaciated until 8 March, when she finally succumbed to the effects of the starvation diet enforced on her by her husband. A surgeon who examined her shortly after her death described her body as 'nothing but skin and bone'.

Tucker stood trial for the wilful murder of his wife at the Wiltshire Assizes held at Salisbury on 31 July 1811. The trial lasted for seven hours in total and the main witnesses for the prosecution were Ann's children from her previous marriage.

In his defence, Samuel Tucker claimed that his wife suffered from a serious disease of the bowels, which prevented him from sleeping with her or associating with her in any way. He ridiculed the idea that he had starved her to death, telling the court that Ann had a voracious appetite and ate insatiably. Her death, he maintained, was entirely down to the medical problem with her bowels.

The jury chose to disbelieve him and, having heard all the evidence against him, almost immediately returned a verdict of 'Guilty of wilful murder'. The judge ordered his execution, stating that his body should afterwards be passed to the surgeons for dissection.

Samuel Tucker received the verdict with the same lack of emotion that he had displayed throughout the trial. However, while at chapel on the day before his scheduled execution, he apparently prepared for his death by making a full confession to the murder of his wife.

He was executed at Fisherton Anger Gaol in Salisbury on Friday 2 August 1811.

2

'GOD BLESS YOU ALL!'

Purton Stoke, 1819

In 2007, the villagers of Purton Stoke in Wiltshire held their first ever Hang Day Fayre, to commemorate the day in 1819 when between 10,000 and 15,000 people descended on the village from far and wide to witness the public hanging of a local ruffian, Robert Watkins.

Stephen Rodway was a successful coal and salt merchant who lived in Cricklade with his wife Mary. His son-in-law, John Habgood, managed his business for him and, between 1 p.m. and 2 p.m. on 7 May 1819, he watched as his father-in-law set off to ride towards Wootton Bassett. Rodway was carrying a good deal of money, including a £5 note and two £1 notes and, as a precaution, Habgood had not only marked the notes for identification, but had also made a note of their serial numbers.

Rodway arrived at Wootton Bassett safely and, having conducted his business there, began his ride home that evening. As he neared the village of Purton Stoke at about 9.30 p.m., a gunshot rang out and, soon afterwards, a man was seen by several witnesses riding through the village on a black horse and turning down Bentham Lane.

About thirty minutes later, Phoebe Grimes was riding along the turnpike road between Purton and Wootton Bassett towards her home in Purton Stoke, when her horse suddenly shied near Moor Stone. Phoebe realised that there was a man lying on the road, apparently dead. She rode as fast as she could to Stoke, where she roused several inhabitants of the village who accompanied her back to the place where she had seen the body. There they found a well-dressed gentleman lying across the road on his back, his arms and legs outstretched. The body was still warm.

One of the men, William Bathe, a solicitor, immediately took charge. He sent for a surgeon and, while waiting for him to arrive, made a quick search of the dead man's pockets to see if anything could be found that might identify him. All that was found was some small change in the pocket of his waistcoat.

William Wells, the surgeon from Cricklade, arrived on the scene at about 11 p.m. and, having pronounced life extinct, ordered the body to be removed to the Bell

The corner near Purton Stoke where Stephen Rodway was killed. (© N. Sly)

public house at Purton Stoke. There he was able to examine the body more closely and found that the man had been shot in the chest, which had one large wound, with two smaller ones at each side. At a post-mortem examination, Wells found that a shirt buckle had been driven into the man's chest with such force that it had ruptured an artery, which Wells believed would have caused instant death. Three horseshoe nails were also found in the body, one lodged in a rib, a second in one of the lungs and the third in the man's spine. From the position of the wounds, Wells surmised that the man had been on horseback when he was shot, but would have been leaning forward, since the bullet had passed obliquely through his body, exiting his back just below his right shoulder blade. The bullet had perforated the man's spine, which also seemed to have been pierced; possibly by two more nail heads.

On the morning after the murder, William Simpkins of Bentham had found a loose horse, which was quickly identified as belonging to Stephen Rodway. The local police called for the assistance of John Vickery, a Bow Street runner, and began to follow up descriptions of the horseman and, before long, they were focusing their attention on twenty-five-year-old Robert Watkins, who lived at Wootton Bassett with his father and sixteen-year-old brother, Edward.

Watkins not only matched the description of the rider but had also been spending money much more freely than normal since the murder. His house was searched, but no incriminating evidence was found there.

Watkins was questioned at Cricklade on 11 and 12 May by John Vickery and members of the local constabulary, in the presence of solicitor Nathaniel Wells, who was later to act as prosecuting counsel at Watkins's trial. Watkins told the police that

The Bell Inn, Purton Stoke. (© N. Sly)

on the evening of the murder he had been drinking in the White Hart until about 8.20 p.m. He had planned to visit his mother, but had changed his mind. He had passed the scene of the murder at about 9 p.m., cutting across a field towards Purton Stoke and going straight home. He had met a man riding a horse by the blacksmith's shop in Purton and the man had a great coat rolled up and secured behind his saddle, as had Stephen Rodway when his son-in-law last saw him. Watkins said that he had met nobody that he knew that night, although he had seen two strangers walking near the school on Purton Hill. He had arrived home just after 10 p.m., having heard the church clock striking moments before he reached his door. He had not heard any gunshots.

Questioned about the money he had been spending, he maintained that it was the remains of the wages he had received for a period of work on the canals near Chichester. When Vickery asked him if he had ever had a pistol in his possession, Watkins said that he had had one, but that he had sold it four or five years previously to a man from Wootton Bassett named Mr Blanchett. Vickery went straight to see Mr Blanchett who told him that, rather than buying a pistol from Watkins, he had sold him one. Confronted with this information, Watkins insisted that the man was mistaken and that he had sold Blanchett his pistol for 4s and a pair of shoes.

Watkins then changed his story and went on to tell Vickery that he had actually heard the gunshot and that he had been near enough to the scene of the murder to see a man riding away on a horse. Although he didn't know the man, he gave the police a description and swore that he would be able to recognise him straight away if he ever saw him again.

The grave of Stephen Rodway, Cricklade. (© N. Sly)

The police rounded up three men who fitted the description that Watkins had given them – Thomas Ockwell, Henry Packer and Henry Ockwell – and brought them before Watkins. Watkins unhesitatingly picked out Thomas Ockwell as the man that he had seen on the night of 7 May. Thomas Ockwell immediately protested that he had been nowhere near the scene of the murder, but had in fact been at Oxford at the time that Stephen Rodway met his death. Vickery was later to take Ockwell to Oxford and came back satisfied that he had a cast-iron alibi.

Robert Watkins was eventually charged with the wilful murder of Stephen Rodway and committed for trial at the next Wiltshire Assizes by the local magistrates. His younger brother, Edward, who was believed to have buried the murder weapon in a ditch, was charged with being an accessory after the fact.

The trial opened at Salisbury before Mr Justice Best at the end of July 1819. There was no direct proof that Edward Watkins had been involved in the murder, so the case against him was dismissed and he was released. Mr Casberd, for the prosecution, then focused on trying Robert Watkins, who pleaded 'Not Guilty' to the charge.

The prosecution produced numerous witnesses who had seen Watkins in the area both immediately before and after the murder was committed and several who had seen him in possession of a pistol, one of whom, James Smith, had actually repaired a pistol for Watkins on 5 May. Henry Cox, a local stonemason, testified to having talked to Watkins at the White Hart Inn at Cricklade at about 8 p.m. Watkins had with him a greatcoat, which he kept rolled up on his knees all evening. William Hicks and Thomas Eagles had been driving sheep on Purton Hill, when a man wearing a greatcoat similar to the one described by Cox had passed them, averting his face as though he wished to avoid being identified.

Ann Seymour testified to hearing the gunshot and seeing a man resembling Watkins riding through the village shortly afterwards, and Phoebe Grimes, William Bathe, William Wells, John Habgood and John Vickery were all called as witnesses for the prosecution, as was James Kibblewhite, who was able to corroborate Thomas Ockwell's alibi.

Mr Casberd then dealt with the money that had been stolen from the victim. He called Mr Edward Belcher, the draper from Wootton Bassett, who produced two £1 notes that the accused had spent at his premises. Thanks to John Habgood having marked the notes and written down their serial numbers, Mr Belcher's notes were indisputably proven to have been among the money carried by Stephen Rodway on the day of his death.

Next, Sophia Cozens took the stand. The daughter of Watkins's landlady at Hunston, where he had lodged while working on the canals at Chichester, she testified to having received two letters from Watkins, both arriving on 12 May. The first letter, dated 8 May, contained a £5 note and instructions for her to buy a sow and pig. The second letter, dated 10 May, told her that there was a problem with the £5 note and asked her to return it to him as soon as possible. Miss Cozens had returned the money to Watkins immediately. The police had intercepted her letter, and found the £5 note to be Rodway's.

The only defence that Watkins could muster was that he knew nothing about the murder, he had not written the notes to Sophia Cozens, and he had never had the £5 note in his possession. The evidence against him was so overwhelming that it took the jury just one minute to return a verdict of 'Guilty', leaving the judge to sentence him to be hanged on the spot where the crime was committed and his body given for dissection.

On 30 July 1819, just two days after the conclusion of his trial, Robert Watkins was transported to Purton Stoke, where a gallows had been erected at Moor Stone. Two hundred special constables had been deputised to control the huge crowd that had assembled to watch the proceedings.

Watkins walked bravely to the gallows, pausing only to shake hands with his mother. He protested his innocence and declined an offer from the Revd Mr Harrison, the prison chaplain, to unburden his soul by confessing his sins. Having mounted the scaffold, he read aloud Psalm 108 then said 'God bless you all!' to the crowd.

It is said that, at the very moment that Robert Watkins met his death on the gallows, a violent clap of thunder exploded and the heavens opened, drenching the crowd with torrential rain. Ironically, Purton Stoke's Hang Day Fayre, originally scheduled to be held on 28 July, near the anniversary of the hanging, was also a victim of the torrential rain and flooding of 2007 and had to be rescheduled to the end of September.

3

'MAY I BE DAMNED TO EVERLASTING IF I HAD ANYTHING TO DO WITH THE HATCHET'

Sutton Benger, 1820

Nobody objected to the gypsies who regularly used Sutton Lane, near Sutton Benger, as their camping ground. Yet one of the gypsies, Edward Buckland – or Buckley as he was sometimes known – was so universally reviled that his own tribe had disowned him because of his evil behaviour. Thus Ted tended to travel the area alone, sleeping under hedges or occasionally in barns when the local farmers took pity on him.

By 1820, Ted was sixty-six years old. A swarthy man, with black hair, grey whiskers and a long beard, he was usually dressed in a dirty old blanket, which he tied around his waist with string.

In the late spring of that year, Ted knocked on the door of Brookside Cottage. The owner, fifty-eight-year-old widow Judith Pearce, who worked at nearby Church Farm, had been known to give Ted a crust of bread in the past. However, on that day, Ted wanted more than just food and asked if he could come into the cottage and warm himself in front of the fire. Not surprisingly, Mrs Pearce refused. Ted went away angry and, later that evening, the thatched roof of the cottage caught fire.

The flames were thankfully extinguished before too much damage was done and it was widely believed that Ted Buckland had started the fire to get his own back on Mrs Pearce for refusing to let him inside her cottage. Ted was quickly apprehended, but he managed to escape his captors and prudently left the area.

Ted was not seen around Sutton Benger again until mid-November 1820. On 12 November, he knocked on the door of a cottage owned by Mrs Ann Flowers, begging for clothes. Mrs Flowers found him a coat and some breeches that had belonged to her husband.

The High Street, Sutton Benger. (Author's collection)

The argument with Buckland earlier in the year had thoroughly unnerved Judith Pearce, hence her twelve-year-old granddaughter, Elizabeth Cottle, had moved in with her to keep her company. In the early hours of the morning of 13 November, Judith and Elizabeth were asleep in Brookside Cottage when they were disturbed by the sound of somebody trying to get into the house.

The frightened woman and child barred the kitchen door then watched in terror as the intruder began to hack through it with an axe. In desperation, Judith Pearce managed to break through the thin lath wall of the cottage and the two escaped through the hole in the wall, into the garden. The intruder followed. He knocked Mrs Pearce down and grabbed Elizabeth, who somehow managed to wriggle free from his grasp. The girl ran as fast as she could through the darkness to her great-uncle's house in the village and roused the occupants. As she was blurting out her story, the church clock struck three.

The girl's two uncles, William and Thomas, her aunt and two neighbours, Daniel Powell and John Price, hurried back to Brookside Cottage, where they found Judith Pearce lying dead in the garden. At a later post-mortem examination, conducted by Dr Joseph Hayward, it was discovered that she had four wounds to her head, caused, the doctor theorised, by her being hit with a blunt instrument. Nothing had been stolen from the house.

The police were called and an immediate search was initiated for Ted Buckland. Not that he took much finding as, early on the morning after Mrs Pearce's death, he was found cooking his breakfast at the side of Sutton Lane. He was immediately arrested and taken before Mr Coleman, the magistrate at Langley Fitzurze, who committed him to stand trial for the wilful murder of Judith Pearce at the next Wiltshire Assizes.

About three weeks after Buckland's arrest, the *Bath Herald* printed an anonymous poem about the murder, clearly assuming that Buckland was guilty, even though his trial had not yet taken place and he was presumed innocent until proven otherwise in the eyes of the law.

A lonely cottage stands beside the way;
A white thatched cot, with honeysuckle gay;
There JUDITH PEARCE, a widow lived alone,
By a rough quarry of blue-coloured stone;
Where lurked a wretch of Egypt's wandering race,
A wretch forlorn, without a mask of grace,
Whom ruffians left, for such a rogue was he,
That even the vilest shunned his company;
Dark was his face but darker still his mind,
To pity, and to every tender feeling blind.
He had no friends, nor knew the joys of home,
But muttering through the dews of night would roam,
Brooding on fancied wrongs with secret pride,
On words, or looks, or benefits denied.
Round his gaunt side a rope for girdle swung,
From which a light, short-handled hatchet hung;
A tattered garment did the village fright,
A coat by day, a blanket all the night,
Which round his neck a butcher's skewer confin'd,
Fit fastening such a filthy dress to bind.
JUDITH had often a kind warning given,
How far his ways were from the ways of Heaven;
And once too, JUDITH (which would kindle strife
In greater persons) asked him –Where's your wife?
Once fire denied, a common courtesy;
Yet there seemed danger in his quick black eye;
And so there was, for as she lay in bed,
At night the thatch was blazing o'er her head.
And EDWARD BUCKLAND, so the villain call,
Was met in haste, close to the village wall;
And if as on some villainy he mused,
The evening salutation he refused;
Suspected, taken, he escapes at last,
And all supposed the danger now was past –
When Judith's brother, in the dead of night,
Heard his grand-niece who shook with cold and fright,
Tell how she 'scaped the murderer's hand by flight;
'Wake! Wake! She's murdered!' was the frightful cry;
'I heard the blow! I almost saw her die.'
They found her lying in the garden mould,
Mangled with dreadful wounds, quite dead and cold.
A sight to shock the weak and almost scare the bold.

THIS STONE
WAS ERECTED BY PUBLIC SUBSCRIPTION
IN MEMORY OF

JUDITH PEARCE

OF THE PARISH OF SEAGRY
WIDOW AGED 58 YEARS
HER BLAMELESS LIFE OF DILIGENCE
AND HONESTY
WAS TERMINATED BY
AN ACT OF THE MOST MALICIOUS BARBARITY
ON THE NIGHT OF 13th NOVEMBER 1820
SHE WAS CRUELLY MURDERED BY
EDWARD BUCKLAND A GIPSEY WHOSE CRIME
WAS PROVIDENTIALLY BROUGHT TO LIGHT
AND HE WAS EXECUTED 17th MARCH 1821

Memorial stone for Judith Pearce, which replaced the original weathered stone. (© N. Sly)

It would have been almost impossible to find anyone to serve on the trial jury that had not previously read the poem and, as a result, formed an opinion on Buckland's guilt.

Buckland's trial opened at Salisbury in March 1821, before Mr Justice Holroyd. The proceedings were constantly interrupted by insane outburst from the accused. Elizabeth Cottle positively identified Buckland as the man who had attacked her and her grandmother, even though it would have been pitch dark at the time and she freely admitted that she hadn't seen her attacker too clearly.

Ann Flowers testified that the coat and breeches that she had given to Buckland had been spotlessly clean. Constable Richard Ellery, who had arrested the prisoner, testified to finding blood and dirt on the clothes, the dirt matching the wattle and daub from the walls of Judith Pearce's cottage.

Almost three months after the murder, Thomas Ferris, the landlord of the Bell Inn, had found a hatchet in a brook in the village. William Greenwood, from nearby Christian Malford, professed to recognise the axe as one that Ted Buckland had tried to persuade him to exchange for a capful of potatoes. Greenwood told the court that he recognised the hatchet as the one that Buckland had tried to swap for potatoes by some letters on the handle. (This was in spite of the fact that Greenwood was completely unable to read or write!) 'May I be damned to everlasting if I had anything to do with the hatchet,' protested Buckland.

He continued to protest his innocence throughout the trial, saying, 'I'll swear upon ten thousand books that I never killed that woman!' However the jury took absolutely no notice and, less than one minute after retiring, returned a verdict of 'Guilty'.

Buckland was executed on 17 March 1821 at Fisherton Anger, the site of the old Wiltshire county gaol, an area now absorbed into Salisbury. It was a double execution, with Buckland, still protesting his innocence, joined on the scaffold by John Asher, who had murdered Patrick MacKay at the Bull Inn, Warminster.

The evidence against Buckland was largely circumstantial, although the fact that nothing was taken from Judith Pearce's home does seem to suggest that someone with a personal grudge against her committed her murder. Since she was known to be a Christian woman of impeccable character, who was well liked by all who knew her, it is difficult to imagine anyone other than Buckland having a motive for the killing. Yet one thing about the case remains puzzling. If Buckland really did kill Judith Pearce, then why was he found calmly cooking his breakfast so close to the crime scene only hours after the murder? If he were the murderer, it seems inconceivable that he should remain in the area, unless he was either so stupid that he just didn't believe that he would ever be connected with her death or so confident that he would be able to talk his way out of trouble. Or was it possible that he knew nothing at all about the murder and was completely unaware that Judith Pearce had been killed?

A frightened child, whom he had attacked in the pitch dark, had verified Buckland's identity, even though she had not seen her attacker clearly. His association with a hatchet, which may or may not have been the murder weapon, was based on identification of letters on its handle by a man who could not read. And his guilt was publicly recorded in the anonymous poem released long before his trial.

4

'I DID IT IN A PASSION, SEEING MY WIFE AND CHILDREN ILL-USED'

Littleton Drew, 1828

As tenants, Robert Brown and his wife and family were simply more trouble than they were worth. They had lived in their house in Littleton Drew for nine years and, throughout their entire tenancy, had paid only £6 in rent. By 1827, their landlord, Richard Lee, had had enough of his unprofitable tenants, who were deeply in arrears with their rent and, thus far, had ignored almost every attempt at communication from Lee's solicitor, John Bush. On the one occasion that Brown had responded to Bush's correspondence, he had appeared in Bush's office in Bradford-on-Avon and argued about Mr Lee's ownership of the property, naming two men, Mr Stone and Mr Henderson, whom he believed had the right to say what he ought to pay.

Finally, Lee himself went to see Brown and offered to waive all of the outstanding rent if Brown and his family would just vacate the house. Brown rejected this offer and, with no other alternative left to him, Mr Lee instructed his solicitor to take the necessary legal measures to evict them.

On 11 April 1828, Sheriff's Officer William Harding went to the house to execute the writ of possession. With him were his assistant, Thomas Sherwood, Mr Lee and his nephew and solicitor John Bush.

They found Robert Brown in the garden and Harding introduced himself, saying that he had come about the business between Brown and Mr Lee. Somewhat indignantly, Brown asked Harding where he came from and on whose authority he was acting. Harding read the warrant out to Brown then went to the door of the house to try and gain entrance.

The door was firmly locked against him and Harding told Brown that he would have to open it. Brown refused, so Harding summoned assistance, which arrived in the person of Thomas Thompson, a local blacksmith, wielding a crow bar, along with a police constable. Between them, the men prised open the door of the house and, with the help of another man, James Clark, set about removing the Brown family's possessions into the road outside.

Once the house was successfully emptied of all furniture and personal effects, John Bush left to return to his office, while William Harding asked Robert Brown, his wife and children to leave the premises, reading the warrant to them once more. They refused, so the assembled men decided to remove them by force.

Mrs Brown was determined that she wasn't going to go quietly and kicked, screamed and struggled as the men attempted to persuade her to go. Eventually William Harding and his assistant each seized one of her arms and briskly propelled her towards the door, with Robert Brown, a child in his arms, obstructing them every step of the way. His wife repeatedly wriggled free from the men's grasp and bolted back indoors before they finally succeeded in removing her. Brown himself was equally vocal, although less violent, and it was between seven and eight o'clock in the evening by the time the family had been completely removed from the house.

As the men stood outside the house with the Brown family, still restraining Mrs Brown to prevent her dashing back inside, Robert Brown suddenly began to rain blows at Thomas Thompson, hitting him three times before turning to Thomas Sherwood and striking him once in the chest. Sherwood immediately turned to Harding and said, 'He has stabbed me!' then Thompson too shouted, 'I am stabbed!' Harding ordered Constable John Daniel to arrest Brown then supported the two injured men into the house, sitting them on the window seat.

A crowd of curious onlookers had assembled outside, one of whom, labourer Richard Walter, later admitted to having moved a short distance away from the house to avoid being called upon to help with the eviction. Now William Harding ran past Walter on his way to summon a surgeon and begged him to go and assist with the two wounded men. Walter went into the house, where he saw both Sherwood and Thompson slumped together on the window seat, 'looking like corpses'. As Walter approached him, Sherwood began to slide off the seat onto the floor. Walter caught him and cradled him in his arms for twenty or thirty minutes until the injured man finally breathed his last.

Thomas Thompson survived the attack after being treated in hospital for three stab wounds – one in the back, one in his right side and the third that went straight through his right arm from one side to another. Surgeon William Fletcher Roberts, who carried out a post-mortem examination on Sherwood, determined that he had died as a result of a single stab wound that was six inches deep and had passed right through his lungs.

At an inquest into the death of Thomas Sherwood, presided over by coroner Mr W. Adye, Robert Brown was committed under the coroner's warrant to stand trial at the next Wiltshire Assizes, charged with wilful murder. The proceedings opened before Mr Justice Park on 23 July 1828, with Mr Bingham prosecuting and Mr Sergeant Mereweather defending.

First to testify was John Bush, who told the court that on 17 September 1827 he had served Brown with notice to quit the house on Lady Day the following year (25 March). Brown had argued that Mr Lee had no right to evict him and that he had been served a notice to quit by another lawyer who had not followed it up.

The Brown family had actually been evicted from the property next door, and seeing that Mr Lee's house was vacant, had decided to move in and squat. According to Brown, Messrs Stone and Henderson owned the house and he paid an annual rent of 1s to the steward of the Duke of Beaufort.

The surviving men who had attempted to evict Brown and his family all gave their accounts of the events of 11 April, along with several men who had visited Robert Brown while he was in custody for the murder. These included Nathaniel Thompson, father of Thomas, who told the court that Brown had apologised for stabbing his son and said that he hoped that Thompson would not die. However, Brown had shown no contrition for stabbing Thomas Sherwood, telling Thompson that he wished he had stabbed two more that were there while he was about it.

Several people had seen Robert Brown produce the murder weapon – an old Spanish bayonet – from his pocket and lunge first at Thompson, then at Sherwood. John Atkins testified to visiting Brown at home two or three years before the murder and complimenting him on his nice house and garden. Brown had told Atkins that he was having a 'disturbance' over it and produced the old bayonet and another instrument, saying, 'If any man do interpose with me again, if one does not do for them, the other should.'

Mr Sergeant Mereweather for the defence objected to the warrant served on Robert Brown by William Harding, pointing out an irregularity in the documentation, which did not correspond exactly with the writ. Mr Justice Park dismissed the objection as irrelevant, saying that even if there had been a trifling discrepancy between the two documents, it did not justify Brown's resistance to being evicted. Finally, the judge asked Robert Brown if he had anything to say in his defence. 'I did it in a passion, seeing my wife and children ill-used,' responded Brown.

The jury returned an almost immediate verdict of 'Guilty' and, when Mr Justice Park passed the death sentence, Robert Brown's lips were seen to quiver slightly, the first sign of any emotion that he had exhibited since the start of his trial. Forty-five-year-old Brown was executed at Fisherton Anger Gaol in Salisbury on 25 July 1828, in the company of the murderer of Sarah Baker (see Chapter 5). Brown's body was handed over to the surgeons to be anatomised. The fate of his 'ill-used' wife and children is not recorded.

5

'THEE WILL BE HANGED IF THEE HAST A HUNDRED NECKS'

On the hot summer morning of 3 July 1828, the hay field was buzzing with rumours about Sarah Baker, who had apparently been unfaithful to her husband some twelve months previously. Unfortunately, the idle gossip reached the ears of Sarah's husband, Nicholas, who promptly stormed home in a rage to find out the identity of the scoundrel who had lain down with his wife.

At about two o'clock that afternoon, Nicholas Baker knocked at the door of the house of his neighbours, Sarah and Thomas Tuck, and told them that a sad misfortune had befallen him. He would not have had it happen for £200, he said, but he had been beating his wife and now feared that she was dead.

Sarah and Thomas Tuck, along with James Buscombe, who was visiting them at the time, hastened to the Baker's home, where they found Sarah sitting up in a chair, wearing nothing but a clean shift and a pair of stockings. She had horrific bruising around her neck and Sarah Tuck later described her badly beaten face as looking 'like a piece of liver'. She was dead.

James Buscombe was immediately despatched to try and find a doctor, Baker followed him a few yards up the road and said, 'Jem, thee wilt be called upon at trial; say the woman was alive when thee came into the house.' Buscombe said that he would do no such thing, telling Baker, 'Thee will be hanged if thee hast a hundred necks.' Baker returned home looking crestfallen. Buscombe had not been walking for long when he met the local surgeon, Mr Edward Spencer, riding his horse along the lane. He led Spencer back to the Baker's home.

When the surgeon arrived, Nicholas Baker had moved his wife from the chair onto the floor, where he had laid her on two sacks. He appeared to have washed the body and attempted to straighten her hair, which Sarah Tuck had noticed was 'very much pulled about' when she first saw the dead woman. Now, Baker was

Lacock village. (Author's collection)

kneeling on the floor, knotting a handkerchief around his wife's jaws to keep her mouth closed.

Mr Spencer examined the body and found two small, contused wounds on the back of Mrs Baker's head. Although her skull wasn't fractured, a large quantity of blood had collected between her brain and her skull and, in Spencer's opinion, this was what had caused her death. In addition, Mrs Baker had extensive blackened bruising to her face, neck, chest, shoulders and upper arms.

Spencer asked Nicholas Baker what had happened and Baker admitted that he had beaten his wife in a fit of jealousy, having heard a woman saying that morning that Sarah had been to bed with another man a year ago. He had confronted Sarah, telling her that if she did not confess the name of her lover, he would give her a devilish good beating. Spencer asked if Sarah had put up any resistance and was told 'none whatsoever'.

Baker willingly produced the very stout stick with which he had hit his wife. He told Spencer that, having started to give Sarah a sound thrashing, he had stopped laying into her for long enough to take her up the back garden to the privy. He had left her there for some time then, when she hadn't come back into the house for him to continue beating her, had gone out to fetch her, finding her partly conscious and incapable of walking. He had dragged her back to the house and put her in the chair, where she had died minutes later, at which he had immediately gone to the Tuck's home for assistance.

The police were summoned and the Lacock officer, PC John Brakeworth, quickly arrived to take Baker into custody. As Brakeworth escorted his prisoner to the police station, Baker told him that, had Sarah not died, he would most probably still be beating her now. He was later to say that it was 'a damned bad job' and that he wished he hadn't done it.

Lacock, 2008. (© N. Sly)

Committed on a coroner's warrant, Nicholas Baker was tried at Devizes on 23 July 1828, his trial immediately following that of Robert Brown, whose story is related in Chapter 4 of this book.

The court heard from Sarah and Thomas Tuck, James Buscombe, Edward Spencer and PC Brakeworth. Baker was not defended, although before the jury retired to consider their verdict, the presiding judge, Mr Justice Park, did give him the opportunity to speak in his own defence. Baker simply muttered something inaudible.

The jury returned almost immediately to pronounce Nicholas Baker guilty of the wilful murder of his wife, Sarah Baker, leaving Mr Justice Park to put on his black cap and decree that Baker should be executed, his body then delivered to the surgeons for dissection. Baker was executed at Fisherton Anger Gaol on 25 July 1828.

It is sadly not unusual for husbands to murder their wives in a fit of jealousy over another man. What makes this particular case different is that, at the time of the murder, Nicholas Baker was seventy-one years old and his wife, Sarah, was sixty-four.

6

'YOU MAY AS WELL LET ME POISON IT'

Warminster, 1830

Harriet Stone and Charles Giles from Whiteparish, near Salisbury, had known each other for seven or eight years and had recently been 'keeping company'. Almost inevitably, Harriet soon fell pregnant. Charles, however, was appalled at the idea of becoming a father and gave strict instructions to Harriet that she was to stifle the child as soon as it was born.

Harriet didn't take him seriously, probably living in hope that Giles would change his mind once the baby was born. Meanwhile, he found her lodgings in Warminster, a suitable distance away from the wagging tongues of their home village, and insisted that she move there. Harriet spent the latter part of her pregnancy alone in her rented room and, when it was time for the baby to arrive, she gave birth with just a nurse in attendance.

However, days after the birth of his son in September 1830, Charles Giles unexpectedly appeared at the window of Harriet's room. Still weak from a difficult confinement, when the nurse brought the baby to Harriet to feed, she promptly passed him to his father to hold. Giles was hardly a proud father. 'What is to be done now the child is living?' he asked Harriet, before disinterestedly handing his son back to her. 'You may as well let me poison it.'

Harriet was understandably distressed at this callous remark, tearfully telling Giles, 'You are not going to poison my child'. Ignoring her tears, Giles left abruptly, returning to Harriet's lodgings within a short while. When she asked him where he had been, he told her that he had been to the top of Cop Heath in Warminster, although he would not say why.

Harriet didn't see her boyfriend again for two weeks, but on 18 September he again knocked on the window of her room. It was about ten o'clock at night and Harriet had already retired to bed but, in response to his knocking, she got up and let him in through the window. Charles told Harriet that he had come to take her home, but Harriet didn't want to leave without paying the nurse the money she was owed for attending the birth and caring for the baby.

Warminster. (Author's collection)

The money due to the nurse was 3*s* 6*d* but Charles told Harriet that he had no small change. Giving her a sovereign, he insisted that she went out herself to get it changed, so she climbed out of the window and went to the house next door. As Harriet knocked on her neighbour's door, she thought she heard her baby give a small, stifled cry. She immediately abandoned her efforts to change the sovereign and went back to her room, having been absent for two minutes at the most.

She had left her son asleep in bed but when she got back, she found Charles holding the infant in his arms. Harriet snatched the baby back and kissed it and as soon as she did, she felt an immediate burning sensation on her mouth. 'Oh my God, Charles, you've poisoned my child,' she shouted at him, but her boyfriend vehemently denied having done anything of the sort. He took his son from her and carefully climbed out of the window, telling Harriet again that he was taking her home and urging her to hurry up and come with him so that they could avoid meeting John Wadley, her landlord, and having to pay her outstanding rent.

Harriet obediently exited through the window and trotted after Charles Giles. When she caught up with him, she slipped her finger into the baby's mouth, finding it to be dry and very hot, the tongue scorched. Harriet immediately sat down in the High Street and closely examined her baby, who had by now drawn his legs up to his stomach and gone limp. Again, she accused Giles of poisoning the child, telling him that the baby was dying, but he continued to deny it. Eventually he grabbed the baby from her, wrapped him in a pillowcase and put the child in the pocket of his smock. He told Harriet that he was going to bury the boy with his brother and that she mustn't say anything to anybody – he then gave her two sovereigns and told her to go and stay with her sister, Mary Ann Rose, in Southampton.

In the event, Harriet initially went to a woman named Phoebe Blake, at whose home she spent the night. The relationship between Harriet and Phoebe is not made clear in the newspapers of the time, although Harriet seems to have told Phoebe that she was a married woman. On the following morning, Harriet got up at five o'clock and set off to travel to her sister's house, first by coach and then on foot.

She arrived at her sister's house in a sorry state. When Mary Ann asked her what the matter was, the story of the death of her baby boy spilled out, in spite of her promises to Charles that she would say nothing. Mary Ann was incensed and persuaded her sister to go with her to see the Mayor of Southampton to lodge a complaint. The mayor directed the two women to the home of a local magistrate but, finding him out when they called, they instead went to the police and demanded that Charles Giles be arrested for the wilful murder of his child.

As a result of the complaint made by Harriet and her sister, Constable Joseph Pizer visited Charles Giles at his home in Whiteparish. Giles initially denied all knowledge of the child but, when his neighbours were questioned, it emerged that he had been seen walking towards a nearby chalk pit with a spade over his shoulder. Pizer went straight to the chalk pit, where he discovered the body of a baby boy buried in a shallow grave.

He immediately took the dead infant to George Nunn, a local surgeon. Nunn conducted a post-mortem examination and noticed that the baby's clothes were 'corroded' in places, as if they had been splashed by acid. The child's lips and left cheek were scorched and, on removing the little boy's clothes, the surgeon found several acid burns on his body.

The baby's stomach contained a quantity of dark liquid, which was so corrosive that it had practically dissolved his stomach and small intestine. When Mr Nunn analysed the fluid, he found it to be sulphuric acid. Since it was impossible for any natural disease to produce sulphuric acid, Nunn concluded that the child had been murdered by the administration of poison.

Charles Giles was committed for trial at the Lent Assizes in Salisbury for the wilful murder of his son. The proceedings opened on 11 March 1831, presided over by Mr Justice Park. Giles pleaded 'Not Guilty'.

The first witness for the prosecution was Harriet Stone, who tearfully related the events of 18 September and also identified the clothes that her baby was dressed in when she last saw him. She wept bitterly as the baby's nightgown, cap, shawl and flannel napkin were produced in court, along with the pillowcase that she had given to Giles to wrap the baby in, which had then become its shroud. Egbert Moon, who had witnessed the opening of the child's makeshift grave by Constable Pizer and the exhumation of the tiny body, testified that they were the clothes that the baby had been wearing when it was found.

Harriet was cross-examined extensively by the counsel for the defence, Mr Dampier, who seemed determined to prove to the court that Harriet and Charles had acted together in killing their illegitimate baby. Dampier asked why Harriet had not told anyone of her boyfriend's insistence that the child should be stifled at birth at the time the threat was made, to which Harriet replied that she had not taken him seriously.

Dampier then called Mary Wadley, the wife of Harriet's landlord, to the stand. Mary had been concerned before the baby's birth that Harriet seemed ill prepared for its arrival. She had suggested that she should buy more baby clothes, to which Mary swore that Harriet had responded, 'Stop and see whether it lives or not, before I get more linen'. Harriet completely denied ever having said anything of the kind. She told the court that she had plenty of things prepared for her baby and that she had been very fond of it and had taken good care of it.

Mrs Wadley also told the court that the child wouldn't suckle, while her husband informed the court that Harriet had escaped through the window of her room to avoid paying her outstanding rent. From his living room, it was possible to hear everything that happened in Harriet's room and, on the night that she had left, he had not heard the baby make any noise at all. Phoebe Blake, with whom Harriet had spent that night, said that, at the time, Harriet did not appear to be in her right mind.

James Dickens, the driver of the coach in which Harriet had travelled to Southampton, testified that Harriet had been carrying a bundle with her throughout the journey and that she had told him that it was a 'bastard child'. According to Dickens, she had pretended to suckle the bundle during the journey, although he had not heard any cries or sounds, nor seen any movement that might have been made by a living child. Dampier pointed out that the implications behind Dickens's testimony were that, although she knew full well that the baby was already dead, Harriet had tried to dupe people into thinking that she was taking her son to Southampton on Monday morning, alive and well.

Dampier also told the court that the baby's nurse had fed it a teaspoonful of poppy syrup about two hours before he died. Harriet argued that the nurse had given the baby poppy oil every night and it had never done him any harm.

Having summoned several witnesses in a vain attempt to blacken Harriet's character, Dampier then produced several more who were prepared to swear to the hitherto unblemished character of Charles Giles. In fact, even the witnesses for the prosecution gave him an excellent character reference, many specifically stating that he had always demonstrated a remarkable fondness for children.

After the judge had summed up the case, the jury retired for only a few minutes before returning with a verdict of 'Guilty of wilful murder' against Charles Giles, although they also made a strong recommendation for mercy, given the prisoner's previous good character and conduct. The judge informed them that, in so atrocious a case, he did not feel inclined to be merciful, then put on his black cap and addressed the prisoner.

He told Giles that he believed that his excellent character was the motive behind what he referred to as 'this most unnatural and inhuman deed'. Mindful of his standing in the local community, Giles had moved Harriet Stone some distance away from her home for her confinement and, once the child was born, had killed it for fear that his reputation would be 'blasted'. It was unthinkable that Harriet should return to their village with an illegitimate babe in arms, since that would destroy Giles' spotless character. Not only that, but Giles had then compounded the offence by trying to insinuate something against Harriet and, furthermore, by trying to make out that she was insane.

'I am innocent', Giles interrupted, but the judge would have none of it.

'Under these circumstances, I dare not, as I tender my duty to God, attend to the kind recommendation of the jury,' he continued, sentencing Giles to be executed and ordering his body to be given to the surgeons for dissection.

Giles promptly burst into tears and 'appeared in great agony of mind'. He was removed from the court, still protesting his innocence, but his protests fell on deaf ears and he was executed at Salisbury on 14 March 1831. After hanging for the customary period of one hour, his body was cut down and, according to the judge's instructions, presented to the surgeons.

7

'OH, MY GOD! I AM A RUINED WOMAN!'

Highworth, 1835

'It was laid down by the law, that if a man found his wife in bed with an adulterer and he put him to death on the instant, the crime was only manslaughter, but if he did this deliberately, and after he had time to think and reflect, the crime would amount to murder'. Such was the legal conundrum put before the jurors in the case of Henry Wynn who, in December 1835, was accused of killing Eliza Jones.

On 7 December, Eliza, an Irishwoman, walked into the beer shop and lodging house owned by Mr Griffith in Highworth. She was accompanied by a blind man and another couple. The group had been sitting in the kitchen of the lodging house for about two hours when another man, Henry Wynn, entered the premises. Walking straight up to the blind man, he said, 'Joe, I don't thank thee for sending me to walk and taking my woman away with thee.'

His words were met with an immediate denial from blind Joe, who assured Wynn that he had not taken Eliza away – in fact he had hardly spoken half-a-dozen words to her. At the same time, Eliza Jones got to her feet and tried to placate her boyfriend, promising him that she was 'not away with anyone' and asking him not to 'fall into a passion'. Her pleas earned her a resounding slap on the face, at which she screamed out in pain and anger. Wynn then pulled a clasp knife from his pocket and told Eliza that he 'had a damned good mind to stab her.'

'Pray don't stab me,' Eliza begged. At this point Sophia Dix, a servant at the beer shop, decided to intervene, telling Wynn to put the knife away. Wynn reassured Dix that he was only intending to scrape some dried mud from his coat and proceeded to do so. Then suddenly, before anyone had time to react, he swung at Eliza, the knife in his hand. The knife went into her left side, at which Eliza cried out, 'Oh, my God! I am a ruined woman!' before collapsing into the arms of the woman with whom she had been drinking for the past couple of hours. Henry Wynn calmly folded up his knife and put it into the pocket of his waistcoat.

Sophia Dix screamed for help and another customer of the beer shop, John Dine, jumped up and bravely approached Wynn, holding out his hand for the knife.

The High Street, Highworth, 1906. (Author's collection)

Wynn meekly passed it to him without comment and Dine tossed it to Sophia Dix for safekeeping.

A surgeon and the police were sent for and Eliza Jones was carried upstairs, where she was made comfortable in one of the lodging house beds. Sophia Dix undressed her, noticing as she did that the knife had penetrated Eliza's stays.

Surgeon William Gane arrived to attend to the wounded woman and found that she had a stab wound on her left-hand side, between her ninth and tenth ribs. At first glance, the wound, which was about an inch long, didn't look too serious to the surgeon, who cleaned and dressed it and promised to call again the following morning. Meanwhile, Henry Wynn was marched off to the poor house, where he was locked up for the night.

Sophia Dix stayed with Eliza Jones until about half-past eleven that night, when her mistress sent her to get some rest. Eliza spent an uncomfortable night, throughout which she constantly insisted that she was going to die.

By the following morning, when Sophia saw Eliza again, it was obvious that her condition had worsened. Mr Gane called again between eight and nine o'clock but there was nothing further that he could do to help Eliza, and she died soon after the surgeon's visit. When Gane later examined her body, he found that Wynn's knife had entered Eliza's side and penetrated to a depth of two and a quarter inches, nicking her colon and causing the contents of her intestines to escape, thus bringing about her rapid death from peritonitis.

Thomas Scaley, the assistant overseer for the parish of Highworth, visited Henry Wynn in custody at the poor house shortly after nine o'clock on the morning of 8 December, asking Wynn if he had heard that Eliza Jones had died. Wynn acknowledged that he had, adding that he had been very sorry to hear it.

The High Street, Highworth, 1915. (Author's collection)

Scaley had then showed Wynn the knife that Sophia Dix had given to him earlier that morning, asking Wynn if he recognised it. 'That was the knife I done the deed with', said Wynn, miming his stabbing action for Scaley. He then explained to Scaley that Eliza Jones had left him and gone away with the blind man, making him so jealous that he had been forced to stab her. Wynn assured Scaley that he was truly sorry for what he had done and that he knew that he must now suffer for it.

Henry Wynn was tried for the murder of Eliza Jones before Mr Justice Littledale. The proceedings were opened and concluded on the same day, 11 March 1836. Given that Wynn had already confessed to the murder, Mr Smith, for the prosecution, merely outlined the facts of the case, calling Sophia Dix, William Gane and Thomas Scaley as witnesses.

Wynn was not defended, although he was allowed to speak in his own defence. He claimed to recall very little about the night of 7 December after taking the knife out of his pocket. He did not remember stabbing Eliza Jones or know how she had died as, at the time of the murder, his reason was quite gone.

After Wynn had spoken, Sophia Dix was recalled to the witness box to add to her testimony with specific regard to Wynn's mental state when he had stabbed his girlfriend. She stated that she didn't believe that Wynn was 'in a passion' and that she didn't think that he was 'tipsy'.

It was then left to Mr Justice Littledale to sum up the case for the jury. Saying that he was sure that the jury would give the case their most serious and deliberate consideration, the judge then informed them that the question was whether the killing of Eliza Jones amounted to the full crime of murder or whether there was anything about the case that could reduce it to manslaughter. Having outlined the law on adultery for them, he pointed out that this only applied if the respective parties were man and wife and there was no evidence that Wynn and Jones had ever been legally married. Thus there were just two points for them to consider – if the accused had occasioned the death of Eliza Jones and, if so, whether he was guilty of murder or of manslaughter.

The jury chose the former option, finding Henry Wynn 'Guilty of wilful murder' and leaving the judge to mete out the prescribed sentence. Wynn was to be executed and his body buried within the confines of the prison. He was hanged just three days later, on 14 March 1836 at Salisbury.

8

'DAMN YOUR EYES, GET UP, OR I'LL KILL YOU DIRECTLY'

Box, 1841

Ann Little was born in Box in 1796, one of three children of James and Ann Little. As a child, she had a quiet, respectable upbringing but, when she was fifteen years old, she moved to London where she 'went on the town' and, by the time she returned to Wiltshire six years later, her character had undergone a complete transformation for the worse.

She took up residence in a house in Kingsdown, Box, in which the other occupants were notorious in the area for their drunkenness, stealing, poaching and loose morals. Before long, Ann was serving a three-month prison sentence, having been convicted of stealing potatoes.

In May 1817, Ann gave birth to an illegitimate daughter, whom she named Grenada. Four years later, she bore a son, George, then another, Thomas, in 1826 then James in 1832. She eventually settled down with Isaac Smith, a widower who was fifteen years her junior. Isaac, known as 'Crafty Ike', is variously described in contemporary newspaper accounts as a mason, a quarryman and a labourer on the railway. He also had four children and, it was rumoured, had starved his first wife to death. By the time he and Ann got together, only two of his boys were still living with him, William, aged fourteen, who worked as a quarryman, and his eleven-year-old brother, Francis, who worked as a farm labourer.

Within two years, Ann gave birth to another baby boy, who was named Isaac after his father. It appears that, soon afterwards, Ann and Isaac senior decided to legalise their union and the banns were called for their wedding. However, the ceremony never actually took place, probably because the couple did not have the money to pay the fees.

On Saturday 4 September 1841, Isaac Smith collected his week's wages and, accompanied by his son William, went straight to the Grove Inn at Ashley to

Ashley, 2008. (© N. Sly)

begin spending them. At about seven o'clock in the evening, they were enjoying their first pint of beer when Ann, Francis and one-year-old Isaac arrived to join them. Ann was already rather drunk and, by the time the family left the inn at nearly eleven o'clock she had consumed about five pints of beer and was extremely intoxicated.

The group walked home together, with Francis carrying baby Isaac, his mother being too drunk to be trusted to carry him herself. Although their house was less than a mile from the pub, Ann kept sitting down at the roadside and claiming that she couldn't walk any further. Isaac Smith repeatedly encouraged her to keep moving by beating her, at which she would reluctantly get up, walk a few steps more, then sit down and refuse to go on. Eventually, Isaac lost all patience and shouted, 'Damn your eyes, get up, or I'll kill you directly'. He then gave her a thorough kicking with his iron-tipped boots, after which he dragged her down the road while Ann pleaded with him, 'Isaac, help me up. I a'nt able to bear it.'[*sic*]

'Don't be so false or I'll throw you into the hedge,' retorted Isaac. Infuriated, he finally gave up his efforts to get her to walk and, leaving her lying on the ground groaning, he and the boys walked home without her.

However, having reached their cottage he found that the door was locked and remembered that Ann had the key in her pocket. Having tried unsuccessfully to kick the door down, he was forced to retrace his steps but, by the time he got back to the place where he had left her, she had disappeared. The first place Isaac thought to look for her was the Swan public house in the village and, sure enough, Ann was there enjoying yet another drink. Once again, Isaac expressed his displeasure at her behaviour with his fists and, this time, he beat Ann so badly that she was unable to walk at all and Isaac was forced to give her a piggyback home. Once there, he threw her down on the floor, sat in a chair by the fire and went to sleep.

He was wakened shortly afterwards by the hungry screams of baby Isaac. Ann was still lying on the floor and Smith shook her and suggested that she suckled the baby at her breast to quieten him. One of the other children managed to prop Ann up enough to be able to feed her baby, while Isaac Smith ate his own supper and then retired to bed.

When he had left the room, Ann's son Thomas helped his mother into the chair by the fire. There was a pool of blood on the floor where she had been lying and the lower half of her gown was saturated with blood – even so, Thomas carried on upstairs to his bed without seeking medical assistance for his mother.

At about four o'clock that morning, he decided to check on her and found her still sitting in the chair exactly as he had left her, only now cold and lifeless. He went straight back upstairs to Isaac's bedroom and told him that Ann was dead; 'Is she?' asked Isaac, disinterestedly. He then went downstairs to look for himself, telling Thomas that he had better go and fetch his uncle, before returning to bed and going back to sleep.

The uncle was summoned and he sent for a surgeon, who determined that Ann Little had been dead for some hours. Her face, body and legs were all severely bruised and there was a long slash in the back of her dress, as well as several lacerations on the lower part of her body, which had apparently been caused by a knife. At a later post-mortem examination, conducted by Mr Goldstone, it was found that Ann Little had bled to death from mainly internal injuries.

Isaac Smith was arrested and charged with wilful murder by PC Thomas Bath of Box. He told the policeman that he had beaten Ann scores of times, but had never believed it would come to this. As he left his house to be taken into custody, he said sadly that he supposed he wouldn't be coming back there again. He said goodbye to his children and told them to mind their uncle.

An inquest was held into Ann's death before coroner Mr W.B. Witmarsh, at which several witnesses were called. One person, whose house stood by the road in Box, testified to seeing Smith dragging Ann Little along and beating her when she fell to the ground from 'exhaustion'. Another, Charlotte Tye, had seen Smith viciously kicking and beating her while she begged him for mercy. A third, James Gale, had heard Ann cry out, 'Oh, my dear Isaac'. He had looked out of the window of his cottage and seen Smith alternately dragging and kicking Ann along the road.

Ann's son Thomas was called to give evidence, but the coroner would not allow him to testify, having discovered that the boy, who was then about fourteen years old, did not understand the concept of swearing an oath. Mr Witmarsh questioned Thomas at length and found that he had never heard of the Bible or God, had never once been into a church or chapel, did not know his catechism, and didn't understand the consequences of telling a lie.

Even without Thomas's testimony, the coroner maintained that, 'Nothing could be clearer or more connected than the evidence adduced,' and the jury agreed, returning a verdict of wilful murder against Isaac Smith, who was sent to Devizes prison to await his trial at the Lent Assizes in Salisbury. Described as a tall, athletic man, Smith was said to have 'preserved the most solid and brutish indifference' to his situation. He insisted that he could recall absolutely nothing of the events leading to the death of his common-law wife.

The trial opened on 3 March 1842 before Mr Justice Coleridge, with Mr Mereweather conducting the prosecution and Mr Edwards defending.

The case unfolded with a repetition of the evidence as it had been presented at the coroner's inquest. Mr Edwards, the defence counsel, tried to convince the jury that, this being a domestic matter between husband and wife, the accused should be tried for common assault rather than murder or even manslaughter. When Mr Justice Coleridge summed up the case for the jury, he explained the difference between murder, manslaughter and common assault and stressed that drunkenness was no excuse in the eyes of the law.

The jury retired to consider their verdict and returned with a verdict of 'Guilty of wilful murder'. However, they were obviously unsure of their decision, since one member of the jury then asked the judge whether it was possible for them to reduce the offence from murder to manslaughter.

Mr Justice Coleridge assured the jury that it was within their power to do so and that the question of whether Smith was guilty of murder or manslaughter was entirely their decision. After a short consultation, the jury decided that manslaughter was the more appropriate verdict, so Isaac Smith escaped the hangman's noose and was instead sentenced to transportation for life.

After a period of detention on the prison hulk *Leviathan*, moored in Portsmouth Harbour, on 26 August 1843 Isaac Smith began the six-month journey on the *Maitland* to Norfolk Island, Van Diemen's Land. He was apparently granted a pardon in 1855, which allowed him to live in Australia as a free man, and eventually died in Hobart, Australia.

9

'THEY SAY I MURDERED MY BABY?'

Westbury, 1849

In 1849, the child mortality rate in England was high and women often had large families in the realistic expectation that not all of the children would survive. More than one in every ten children died in the first year of their lives and many more did not reach their fifth birthday. That said, Rebecca Smith seemed to have been unluckier than most women; having given birth ten times, no less than nine of her babies had died, usually when they were around one month old.

To all intents and purposes, Rebecca was a God-fearing Christian woman, a regular attendee of Divine Worship at chapel, who was in the habit of saying her prayers every night. Ann Newman, a fellow chapel-goer, described her as a 'well-conducted, industrious woman of a kind, quiet disposition.'

By 1849, Rebecca, who was in her forties, had been married to Philip Smith for eighteen years. Philip was a very heavy drinker, who, over the course of their marriage, had squandered a £100 inheritance that Rebecca had received from her father. The couple, who had one living daughter, rented a 30-acre smallholding in Westbury and Philip worked sporadically as a labourer to support his family.

On 16 May, Rebecca gave birth to her eleventh baby, a son whom she named Richard. Her friend, Elizabeth Cockle, who was present at the birth, described the infant as a fine, healthy, full-term baby boy.

Elizabeth was in and out of the Smith's home every day for the next few weeks, during which time the baby appeared to thrive, although he did develop some small boils on his ears shortly after birth, which disappeared of their own accord in a couple of days. However, on 10 June, she noticed that baby Richard was not at all well, having vomited something that resembled the yolk of an egg. Elizabeth was of the opinion that the child 'had bile' and, since the baby was so sick, she advised Rebecca to consult a doctor. 'It is no good to apply to any doctor for such an infant,' was Rebecca's response. She didn't mention to Elizabeth that she had already consulted a doctor about the baby on 8 June.

Two views of Westbury, 2008. (© N. Sly)

Henry Britton, a surgeon from Bratton, had met Philip Smith on the evening of 5 June. Philip had expressed some concerns about the health of his wife and son and, as a consequence, Britton had agreed to examine them. He found baby Richard to be a normal, healthy baby, in spite of the fact that the baby's mother assured him that the child had been ill. At Britton's visit, Rebecca herself complained of feeling weak and of having been sick. Unable to find anything much wrong with her, Britton simply advised her to make sure that she was eating properly.

At six o'clock on the morning of 12 June, Elizabeth Cockle was summoned urgently to Rebecca Smith's home, where she discovered that baby Richard had died. Elizabeth helped her friend to lay out the baby, giving her a little cap that had belonged to one of her own children to cover a sore on the back of his head. Having washed the child and dressed it in clean linen, she placed the body in a tiny coffin, Rebecca warning her not to turn the baby over as she did or 'something would run from its mouth'. The baby was buried in the graveyard at Bratton Baptist Chapel.

However, there were those in Westbury who nursed suspicions about the sudden death of Richard Smith and rumours began to circulate throughout the town that Rebecca had killed her baby. Before long it became impossible for the authorities to ignore the buzz of gossip and it was decided to exhume the baby and carry out a post-mortem examination on his remains. Accordingly, Humphrey Newman, the sexton at Bratton, was given instructions by the coroner to dig up the recently buried coffin, which he did on 22 June, handing it straight to PC James Burgess, the Westbury constable. Burgess took the coffin to the Lopes Arms public house and locked it up, giving the key to surgeon George Sharland, who was also the registrar of births and deaths for the area. Sharland had met Rebecca Smith on two previous occasions, when she had registered first the birth, then the death of her son. On the latter meeting, he had asked her if any surgeon had attended her baby before its death and had been told that Mr Britton had seen Richard.

On 23 June, Mr Sharland and a colleague, Mr J.H. Gibbs, went to the Lopes Arms and opened the coffin. Elizabeth Cockle was present and formally identified baby Richard, pointing out the little cap that she had placed on his head only a few days before. An initial examination of the tiny corpse showed that Richard seemed to have been a normal, healthy, well-nourished baby, although he had a small sore on the back of his head. Yet when the surgeons opened up his body, they noticed some inflammation and ulceration of the stomach and intestines. They removed the fluid contents of the stomach and subjected them to various chemical tests, all of which indicated the presence of metallic arsenic. Sharland and Gibbs jointly formed the conclusion that baby Richard had died as the result of arsenic poisoning.

At an inquest into baby Richard's death, held at the Lopes Arms, the coroner's jury recorded a verdict of wilful murder against Rebecca Smith and she was committed for trial at the next Wiltshire Assizes.

Her trial at Devizes was presided over by Mr Justice Cresswell, with Mr Slade and Mr Lopes prosecuting and Mr Haddow acting as defence counsel. The courtroom was packed with spectators, all eager to hear the gruesome details of the case.

First to testify was Elizabeth Cockle who told the court that she had seen Richard every single day of his life and that he had been a normal, healthy baby until shortly before his death. Rebecca Smith had complained that the baby cried

The Lopes Arms, Westbury, 2008. (© N. Sly)

excessively at nights and Elizabeth, herself the mother of three children, had recommended giving him syrup of rhubarb.

Several people then testified to the fact that Rebecca Smith had bought arsenic shortly before baby Richard's death. The first of these was fourteen-year-old Charlotte Mackey, who occasionally ran errands for Rebecca. Charlotte told the court that Rebecca had sent for her on 27 May and asked her to go to Mr Taylor, the druggist in Westbury. She wanted her to buy a pennyworth of poison for rats and mice that she could send to her sister, whose house in Bratton was troubled with vermin. Charlotte had taken the penny and gone to her mother, who told her that she would not be allowed to buy poison without a witness, so Charlotte had returned the money.

On 7 June, Prudence Mead had met Rebecca in the street and, knowing that she had recently had a baby, asked her how she was. Rebecca said that she felt very poorly and wanted to sit down somewhere, so was invited into the Mead's home. There she told Prudence that she had come into town in order to visit Mr Taylor's shop to buy a pennyworth of poison, saying she couldn't put anything out of her hands at home for the mice. She asked Prudence if she would accompany her, as she had been told that she wouldn't be allowed to make her purchase without a witness present. Prudence went with Rebecca to Mr Taylor's shop and heard her ask the apprentice, Alfred Mumford, for a pennyworth of poison to kill mice. She was asked what sort she wanted and replied that she didn't know.

Mumford was called to testify and described taking down a bottle of white arsenic from a shelf and suggesting that it would suit her purposes. He weighed the arsenic onto a piece of blue paper, on which he wrote 'Arsenic. Poison'. He then warned Rebecca Smith that it was highly dangerous and that she should take particular care to keep it away from children. Rebecca assured him that she intended to send the poison to her sister in Bratton and was not going to use it herself.

The next witness to be called was midwife Jane Harris, who had attended Rebecca at Richard's birth. Harris had not been paid for her services and had called on Rebecca several times in an effort to get her to settle her outstanding account. She described baby Richard as a beautiful, healthy baby and stated that she had told Rebecca that she hoped that this child would survive, unlike her previous babies. On Harris's next visit, Rebecca had asked her if she thought the baby 'did worsty' [sic]. Harris had assured her that the baby was growing normally but when she called again on 25 May, Rebecca had again asked her if the child 'did worsty', telling the midwife that baby Richard cried a lot and seemed terribly cross. By the time Jane Harris visited Rebecca Smith again, Richard was dead. Rebecca still had no money to pay her bill, but promised she would get it by the next day. Harris had then told Rebecca that she had heard rumours that Rebecca had murdered her baby.

'They say I murdered my baby?' asked Smith incredulously. 'Who told you?'

Harris had named Elizabeth Cockle and Hannah Bailey and told Rebecca that she knew that she had sent Charlotte Mackey to try and buy poison. Rebecca insisted that the poison had been for her sister to kill mice and rats. Harris then accused her of buying poison herself, to which Rebecca indignantly replied that she hadn't been into town since the birth of her baby.

Ann Callaway, Rebecca's sister, was called to testify that, although she had once had a problem with rats and mice at her home, her husband had taken care of it. She had never asked Rebecca to buy or send her any poison and had never heard Rebecca complaining of rats and mice at her own home. This was later confirmed by Sarah Millard, a lodger at the Smith's home for three months until 17 June, who stated that she had never known there to be any problem with vermin in the house. Ann also told the court that her sister's husband was not very kind to her and that the Smith's were very badly off financially. She had taken both food and money to her sister, but insisted that, in spite of her poverty, Rebecca was taking the best possible care of her child.

The prosecution then produced a witness who testified that Rebecca Smith had tried to obtain poison even before the birth of her baby. Jane Joyce had been visiting her sister Hannah Bailey on 24 April when Rebecca Smith had arrived. Rebecca had asked Hannah if she could spare a little bit of poison, as she had a problem with mice at home. Hannah had no poison in the house to give her. Jane, who lived close to the Smith's home, had often seen Rebecca and baby Richard, whom she described as 'a fine healthy child'. On 11 June, she and Hannah had seen Richard again and noticed that he was very pale. Rebecca told her that the baby had been sick during the night. At that time, Hannah suggested that Rebecca gave the baby something to comfort it, but Rebecca said it would be no use.

Hannah had run to her own house and made up some arrowroot for the baby, but Rebecca told her that the child wouldn't eat it. Jane lifted the boy onto her lap and tried to feed him with the arrowroot, which Richard had taken greedily, although he had kept his tongue to the roof of his mouth while eating. Jane also fed some of the arrowroot to her own child at the same time. Hannah found some white ointment that she had bought from Mr Taylor the druggist, which Jane applied to the sore on baby Richard's head, leaving the remaining ointment with

Rebecca to use later. Apprentice Alfred Mumford was recalled to the witness box to testify to the content of the ointment, which he described as 'white lead ointment', specifying that it contained no arsenic.

The next witnesses to be called by the prosecution were those involved with the exhumation of the baby and his subsequent post-mortem examination. Having heard from sexton Humphrey Newman and Constable Burgess, and the surgeons who had carried out the post-mortem examination, the court was then addressed by William Herapath, an eminent Bristol chemist, who had analysed the baby's stomach contents and examined portions of his intestines. He concurred with the surgeons, attributing the baby's death to arsenic poisoning.

Having heard all the evidence presented in court, the jury retired for about thirty minutes, returning with a verdict of 'Guilty of wilful murder' against Rebecca Smith, but strongly recommending mercy for her. When Mr Justice Cresswell asked them on what grounds, they told him that they wished her to have time to repent. Cresswell ignored the recommendation, sentencing Rebecca Smith to death without hope of mercy. She didn't even flinch as she learned her fate.

While confined in the county gaol awaiting her execution, Rebecca Smith confessed to the prison chaplain that she had previously murdered seven of her other children in exactly the same manner as she had killed baby Richard. The only motive that she could offer was that she was afraid that her children might 'come to want'. There were suspicions that she might also have attempted to poison her one living child, but she vehemently denied this, expressing great affection for the child coupled with concerns that, being given to drunkenness, her husband would most probably neglect her daughter after she had been executed.

A petition was raised appealing to the Secretary of State for clemency for Rebecca Smith but it was to no avail. The government declined to intervene in the sentence and Rebecca Smith was executed at Devizes on 23 August 1849.

10

'BEAT THE OLD BASTARD'S BRAINS OUT!'

Trowbridge, 1854

The argument started between two brothers, James and Dennis Napper, and it quickly escalated into a physical fight. The boys' father, Daniel, stepped in to try and separate his sons, much to the disgust of James, who felt that his father was taking sides against him.

The following evening, 31 August 1854, Daniel and his wife Mary Ann went out drinking in Trowbridge with twenty-three-year-old James. James's anger at his father spilled over and the boy began taunting Daniel, hurling insults at him, rolling up his sleeves and putting up his fists as if to fight him. Before long, the fight became reality, as James threw a punch at his father, hitting him squarely in the face and knocking him to the ground. As Daniel lay helpless, James delivered a few well-aimed kicks to his ribs and sides, continuing to swear at his father and threatening to kill him. His mother, Mary Ann, enthusiastically egged him on, telling James to 'Kill the old bastard!' and urging him to 'Beat the old bastard's brains out!' She eventually joined in the fight herself, grabbing Daniel's hair and using it to bang her husband's head repeatedly on the road, all the while swearing that she would murder him.

By now, Daniel was practically insensible but James and Mary Ann hadn't finished with him. James grabbed his father by his shoulders and roughly pulled him into a sitting position, telling him, 'Wake up, you sleepy old bastard'. Rather than helping his father to his feet, James then gave him a violent shove backwards so that Daniel's head once again hit the ground hard.

The attack on Daniel Napper took place in front of several bystanders, all of whom were later to say that it happened so quickly that they had little chance to go to his aid. One man, cloth worker James Brown, did try to help, kneeling on the ground and gently lifting Daniel half upright. However, even while Daniel was

Fore Street, Trowbridge. (Author's collection)

cradled in Brown's arms, his son was still attempting to hit him and threatening to give anyone who took his father's part a good hiding.

Eventually, James and Mary Ann were pulled away from their victim and walked off homewards, leaving Daniel lying where he had fallen. They had only gone a few yards when they stopped and turned round to yell a few more threats that if Daniel came home that night they would finish him off.

With the violent and unpredictable James and Mary Ann out of the way, the witnesses rushed forward to help Daniel to his feet. After resting for a short while, he tried to walk home but had only taken a couple of steps when his legs buckled beneath him and he staggered and fell. He was helped to his feet again and escorted home. Surprisingly, Mary Ann and James didn't carry out their threat to finish him off but allowed him inside the house and put him to bed.

By the following morning, it was only too obvious that Daniel had been very severely injured in the fight. Mary Ann sent for a surgeon, Mr Stapleton, but by the time Stapleton arrived, Daniel was already dying. At a later post-mortem examination it was found that, as well as severe bruising all over his body, Daniel had a fracture at the base of his skull and a ruptured artery

An inquest was opened and the coroner heard from the many people who had witnessed the attack on Daniel Napper, including William Pearce, who had been walking by when the fight had occurred and Mr John Mayell, the landlord of the Bear Inn, outside whose premises the attack had taken place. Once all the evidence had been presented, the coroner looked to the inquest jury for a verdict. They were unable to agree. Of the thirteen-man jury, six were for wilful murder while the remaining seven argued for a verdict of manslaughter against both James and Mary Ann Napper. The jury were completely deadlocked and neither side were prepared to concede.

The coroner took the unusual step of ordering the jury to be locked up overnight but, by the next morning, the split between them remained the same and they insisted that they would be unable to reach a compromise. The coroner was eventually forced to discharge the jury, even though they had failed to reach agreement, and pass the case onto the magistrate's court. There, just two days later, the witnesses gave their evidence again and the magistrates determined that the two accused should stand trial at the next Wiltshire Assizes. The charge against them was to be wilful murder.

The trial opened at Salisbury in March 1855, before Mr Justice Erle, with Mr Hodges prosecuting. Once again the court heard from the numerous people who had witnessed the attack, including James Brown, William Pearce and John Mayell. They also heard from the surgeon, Mr Stapleton, who testified to the extent of Daniel Napper's injuries and the cause of his death.

Once all the evidence had been heard, Mr Justice Erle summed up the case for the jury, paying particular attention to explaining the difference between murder and manslaughter to them. The jury retired only briefly before returning to pronounce both defendants 'Guilty of manslaughter.'

The judge deferred his decision on sentencing the prisoners for a few days, eventually deciding that James Napper should be imprisoned for eighteen months and Mary Ann for six months.

The Napper's were a notorious family who, at the time of the fatal attack on the head of the family, were very much feared in the Trowbridge area. Son Dennis Napper had just returned from transportation, while the victim, Daniel, had also been transported for theft in his youth. In 1839, Daniel himself had been tried for the murder of William Bishop, a common peddler. He had been extremely fortunate to escape conviction because of a minor legal error in the indictment. When the local newspaper printed an account of the murder, they wrongly reported that prior to the fight the Nappers had been drinking in the Bear Inn at Trowbridge. They were quick to retract this statement, presumably at the instigation of landlord John Mayell, who, according to the newspaper was 'naturally desirous to remove the impression that such a decidedly bad lot as the Napper family were numbered among his customers.'

11

'PARDON ME'

Tollard Royal, 1859

On Thursday 3 November 1859, George Trowbridge ate breakfast with his wife Anastasia as usual and kissed her goodbye before walking the half-mile path to his work. It was to be the last kiss he and his wife would share. When he returned to their cottage in Ashcombe Wood, Tollard Royal for lunch, he found the door locked against him. Looking through the window, he could see Anastasia lying on the floor, her head resting against the wall at an unnatural angle and one arm propped on a chair.

Trowbridge's first reaction was to scream very loudly, attracting the attention of their nearest neighbour, Mrs Parsons, who hurried to see what the matter was. By the time she arrived, George had managed to climb through a back window of the cottage and was sitting on the floor, cradling his dead wife in his arms.

Anastasia had been attacked and now lay surrounded by a large pool of blood. A doctor was summoned and, when Mr Foot the surgeon arrived from Ludwell, he found the dead woman to have been dreadfully mutilated, with numerous wounds to her face and head. Her body was still warm and he concluded that she had been dead for about two or three hours. Dr Richard Shittle, of Cann, near Shaftesbury, later carried out a post-mortem examination and catalogued her terrible injuries. He determined that Anastasia had first been viciously beaten about the head and face. She had lost several of her teeth and many of her facial bones were fractured.

Once she had been rendered unconscious, her attacker had seized a saw from the cottage and proceeded to saw at her head, penetrating her skull in several places and causing horrific damage to her brain.

The saw was left at the cottage, its blade covered with blood, brain matter and hair. A razor was also found in two pieces, the handle on the threshold of the cottage and the blade outside, close to the front door, although only one wound – a clean cut across Anastasia's knuckles – appeared to have been inflicted with a razor. The house had been ransacked and a large chest that stood by the bed upstairs had been broken open, its contents scattered around the room. George Trowbridge was able to tell the police that a number of items of his clothing had been stolen. In all, two coats, three waistcoats, a pair of leggings, a pair of boots and an umbrella were missing from his bedroom.

The police searched the cottage and found that the outside of the front door was heavily blood spattered and that there were large quantities of blood stretching from the door to the place where Anastasia lay. They concluded that she had been initially attacked while she was outside, close to the front door and then dragged inside, where her attacker had savagely mutilated her in the relative privacy of the fairly isolated cottage.

Once the police began their enquiries, they quickly learned that a stranger had been observed loitering in the area for several days before the murder. Numerous people gave the same description of a man who was around thirty years old, 5ft 7in tall, slender, with a dark complexion and a pronounced foreign accent.

Alice Stingimore of Alvedistone had encountered him four days before the murder when he knocked at the door of her cottage and asked in broken English for a bit of bread. She particularly remembered the man because her children had initially answered the door to his knock and had been unable to understand what he was saying. She added that the man was carrying a bundle tied up in dirty blue cloth.

James Stracey, bailiff to Lord Rivers at Rushmore Lodge, recalled that, three days before the murder, the man had been wearing a 'wide awake' hat and, on the same day, Caroline Parsons remembered him coming to the door of her workplace, Ashcombe House, and begging for food.

Three people had seen him at Berwick-St-John on the Tuesday before the murder and all remembered his dirty blue bundle. Nothing was seen of him on the following day, but, on the morning of the murder, Samuel and George Bench had seen him about 300 yards from the Trowbridges' cottage, still wearing his hat and still carrying his bundle.

Armed with these descriptions, the police began an extensive manhunt involving officers from several areas. The cottage was almost on the county border with Dorset and police from both Dorset and Hampshire joined the officers from Wiltshire, led by Superintendent Harris of Hindon, scouring the country night and day in search of the foreign tramp.

Within a couple of hours of the murder, the man had been spotted near the Blandford toll gate and, with the aid of many more witnesses, the police tracked him through Wareham, across Dorset and into Hampshire. There, the tramp had walked through the New Forest towards Southampton.

As he went, he disposed of some of the spoils of the robbery. On the day after the murder, he sold a pocket-handkerchief to Mr Green, a labourer at Piddletrenthide, Dorset. A waistcoat was sold to another man and, on the Monday after the murder, John Jeffreys of Church Knowle paid him 2s for another waistcoat and a necktie. In the New Forest, the tramp called at a public house in Fawley, where the owner, Mr Richard Martin, parted with 7s for a blue coat.

Eight days after the murder, a sharp-eyed policeman, Sergeant Cook, thought he spotted the fugitive at Hythe on the south-western bank of Southampton water. The man boarded a ferry and Cook followed. By the time the ferry reached Southampton, Cook was absolutely positive that he had his man. He arrested him and returned him to Hythe police station for questioning.

The High Street, Hythe, in the late 1950s. (Author's collection)

The man gave his name as Serafin Manzano. A Spaniard, he spoke very little English but Sergeant Cook was able to establish that he had arrived in England from Boulogne. When Manzano was searched, it was found that he was wearing two pairs of trousers and that the outer pair appeared to be bloodstained. He also had a recent cut on the middle finger of his right hand.

A message was despatched to Hindon and Superintendent Harris set out for Hythe immediately, accompanied by George Trowbridge. Trowbridge was able to identify several items of his clothing found in Manzano's possession, including a hat, coat, leggings and the umbrella. The coat was particularly unique, since it had been presented to Trowbridge by the Sturminster Agricultural Society. Manzano had cut off the very distinctive buttons.

Manzano's clothes were sent for testing and he was taken back to Hindon, appearing before magistrates there on 23 November. As he spoke only a little English, Sir G. Cornewall-Lewis, the Secretary of State, made arrangements for an interpreter to attend. Due at the court at eleven o'clock, the interpreter had still not arrived at two o'clock, by which time the magistrates were beginning to tire of waiting for him. A member of the Spanish Consulate in London was attending court and he was asked to act as interpreter for the prisoner – he agreed and the case finally commenced. (The official interpreter finally arrived at 4 p.m., just as the case was closing.)

Through his newly-appointed interpreter, Manzano explained that he had spent many years serving in the Queen of Spain's Army and had arrived in England earlier in 1859 and spent some months travelling around Wales on foot. He denied any involvement in the murder of Anastasia Trowbridge, saying that he had bought the clothes from another tramp, a Pole, who had recently arrived in England from Boulogne.

However, by now analytical chemist Mr William Herapath had examined Manzano's clothes and determined that there were twelve distinct spots of blood, which appeared to have spurted rather than dripped onto his trousers. There were also traces of blood on his shirt, although the garment appeared to have been recently washed.

Mr George Chitty, a solicitor from Cann, near Shaftesbury had been appointed by the court to defend the itinerate Manzano and he assured the court that his client was confident that he could prove that he hadn't been involved in the murder. However, given the evidence of Mr Herapath and the chain of witnesses across three counties who were able to associate Manzano with items stolen from the Trowbridge's home, the magistrates had no hesitation in committing him to stand trial at the next Wiltshire Assizes.

The trial at Winchester was virtually a repeat performance of Manzano's appearance before the magistrates at the Hindon Petty Sessions. Once again, the court heard evidence from witnesses who had bought stolen items from the accused as he walked across the country and their testimonies, coupled with Mr Herapath's report, ensured that the jury ignored Manzano's protestations of innocence to find him guilty of the wilful murder of Anastasia Trowbridge. He was sentenced to death and despatched to Devizes Gaol to await his fate.

Once he was incarcerated in the condemned cell, prison authorities made every effort to ensure that he was as comfortable as possible under the circumstances. This included the provision of a spiritual advisor. The Mayor of Devizes, Mr Burt, fortunately understood some Spanish and managed to elicit the information from Manzano that he was a Roman Catholic and wished to speak with a priest. This was duly arranged and an image of the Virgin and Child procured for his cell.

In the days prior to his execution, Manzano, who was described in contemporary newspapers as 'a quiet, gentle man', drew great comfort from his religion. He gradually revealed a little of his background to prison staff, telling them that he was the son of a Spanish millionaire who owned two silver mines and that he had two sisters, both of whom were nuns who lived in a convent. He told prison officers that God had chastised him for disobeying his father.

Shortly before his death, Manzano wrote two letters. One was to Mr Alexander, the prison governor, thanking him and his wife for their kindness towards him while he was imprisoned. He assured them that he had never committed any crime. He then wrote a letter to the governor's children, advising them to always be obedient to their father.

On the eve of his execution, Manzano slept badly, refusing breakfast when he awoke and accepting only a few sips of tea. At about 11.30 a.m. on 11 April 1860, he was asked if he had any statement or request to make before meeting his death. Manzano stated that he wished for nothing more than the prayers of those assembled and continued to protest his innocence of the murder of Mrs Trowbridge. He was escorted to the gallows where, having stood for almost ten minutes while the Catholic rite of Plenary Indulgence was administered, he made one last desperate appeal to the officials, asking them to 'Pardon me'. His plea was in vain and, seconds later, he died instantly at the hands of the executioner, William Calcraft.

12

'I HAVE DONE IT. YOU HAD BETTER LOCK ME UP'

Devizes, 1881

The infirm ward at Devizes Workhouse was normally a peaceable place, its seven or eight elderly occupants given to sitting around the fire smoking their pipes and chatting. On 24 November 1881 it was a particularly cold day and the seat closest to the fireplace in the ward was very much sought after.

At about nine o'clock in the morning, two inmates started an argument about which of the two of them should occupy a stool by the fire. Sixty-nine-year-old Charles Gerrish, a former labourer, had the upper hand, being in actual possession of the stool at the time. However, seventy-seven-year-old Stephen Coleman was anxious that everyone should have his turn sitting close to the fire. 'You old *******,' he eventually shouted at Gerrish. 'It shall go near the fire and all shall have a hand.' With that, he withdrew to the other side of the room and lit his pipe.

Gerrish meanwhile pushed the poker between two bars of the grate, using it to lift the coals and encourage the fire to burn brighter. He too lit his pipe and sat brooding quietly and smoking for about five or six minutes.

Suddenly, without any warning, Gerrish seized the red-hot poker from the fire, rushed across the ward to where Coleman was still sitting smoking and plunged the poker into his neck. Richard Hayward, with whom Coleman had been quietly chatting, tried to grab Gerrish, who immediately pulled the poker out of Coleman's neck and thrust it at Hayward. Fortunately for Hayward, the poker passed through his clothes without making contact with his body. Hayward and Gerrish struggled for a few minutes, with Hayward sustaining some burns to his hands from the still hot poker before finally managing to disarm his assailant.

With Gerrish subdued and Coleman lying dreadfully injured on the floor, blood pouring from his mouth, someone was sent to fetch workhouse master Henry Hassall and surgeon Mr Waylen. The former arrived at the ward to find an

The assize court in Northgate Street, Devizes, c. 1920. (Author's collection)

unrepentant Charles Gerrish who told him, 'I have done it. You had better lock me up.'

The surgeon arrived within ten minutes of being summoned, but was sadly too late to save the life of Stephen Coleman. At a post-mortem examination it was found that the poker had entered Coleman's neck about three quarters of an inch below the angle of his jaw, leaving a single wound three quarters of an inch long and half an inch wide. The red-hot instrument had penetrated to a depth of several inches, severing some of the main arteries and, as a result, the old man had bled to death.

The police were sent for and Inspector Bull escorted Gerrish to the local police station, where he was charged with the wilful murder of Stephen Coleman. Gerrish seemed totally indifferent to the charge and was described as being 'little affected' by what had occurred. At an inquest held the following day, the coroner's jury recorded a verdict of 'wilful murder' against Charles Gerrish, who was committed on a coroner's warrant to stand trial at the next Wiltshire Assizes.

His trial opened at Devizes before Lord Chief Justice Coleridge in January 1882. Mr Lopes prosecuted and Mr Mathews was requested by the judge to watch the case on behalf of the defendant.

The prosecution began by relating the events of 24 November, calling Richard Hayward as the first witness. Hayward's testimony was corroborated by George Porter, Thomas Butt and Richard Abrahams, three other inmates of the workhouse who had been present in the 'old man's ward' at the time of the murder. The court then heard from Mr Hassall and the surgeon, followed by Inspector Bull of Devizes who had arrested and charged the defendant. At this, the prosecution rested their case.

Mr Mathews argued for the defence that no quarrel was known to exist between the two men prior to the murder. Coleman, who was a long-term inmate at the workhouse, was said to have been of an amicable disposition while Gerrish, who had been a resident for only three months, was also not known to 'be addicted to fits of passion'. Mathews maintained that, immediately before the murder, Charles Gerrish had been greatly provoked by the victim and because of this the jury would be justified in returning a verdict of manslaughter rather than one of wilful murder.

In summing up the case for the jury, Lord Chief Justice Coleridge told them that, in order to reduce the charge from murder to manslaughter, it was necessary that the blow that caused Coleman's death should follow closely after the alleged provocation and that such provocation must be active and not passive. Mere words between the two men would be classed as passive provocation and there was evidence that Gerrish had deliberately waited for five or six minutes to allow the poker to become red hot before his fatal attack on Coleman. The facts of the case, continued Coleridge, were very clear and very simple and the jury should have no difficult in arriving at a verdict. They had a painful duty to perform, but it was a duty that they owed to the general public and they should perform it to the best of their ability.

After a short consultation, the jury returned a verdict of 'Guilty of wilful murder' against Charles Gerrish and, putting on his black cap, the judge addressed the prisoner, telling him that he had been justly convicted. He had sent an old man out of this world into the next without any preparation by a very cruel death and that the act had, on Gerrish's part, been deliberately premeditated. Sentencing Gerrish to be executed, the judge remarked that, unlike his victim, Gerrish would at least have the chance to prepare for his end.

Gerrish accepted his sentence without emotion and was executed at Devizes by William Marwood on 31 January 1882.

[Note: In various accounts of the murder in contemporary newspapers, the name of the doctor originally called to attend Mr Coleman is given as Mr Carloss, Mr Swithin Waylen and Mr George Waylen. Records show that a Mr George S.A. Waylen, with the middle name of Swithin, was practising medicine in Devizes at the time of the murder. Pauper Richard Hayward is also alternatively named Richard Hartward.]

13

'I INTENDED NO HARM TO MY OLD FATHER'

When John Horton's wife fell ill with a bout of the fever, Charlotte Lindsey (aka Charlotte Tarrant) was engaged to nurse her. When Mrs Horton and one of John's eleven children finally succumbed to the illness, Charlotte was obviously a great comfort to the widower, since the couple then cohabited for several years. However, on 17 October 1885, something brought about the end of the relationship and Charlotte moved out of the home that she shared with John at Elms Cross and into a house at Tory, Bradford-on-Avon. At around the same time, she seems to have begun an intimate relationship with Edward, John Horton's sixty-nine-year-old father.

To say that John Horton was furious is an understatement. His jealousy simmered for a few weeks, before finally boiling over on the night of Friday 20 November 1885.

On that night, Edward Horton and Charlotte Lindsey had gone for a drink at the Three Horse Shoes in Bradford-on-Avon. Lindsey left quite early, leaving Edward Horton still drinking and before too long, John Horton arrived at the pub. Edward offered to buy his son a drink and two pints of beer were brought to them, but it was not long before father and son began an argument that so was loud that a passing police officer took it upon himself to intervene and caution both men. The quarrelling men quietened down immediately but soon afterwards John Horton began to insult his father once more, telling him that he had heard that the old man had been thrown out of some very disorderly houses in Trowbridge and saying that someone had offered him a pint of beer to visit the Three Horse Shoes to see with his own eyes what sort of company Edward was keeping. The argument escalated to such a pitch that William Stokes, the pub landlord, was forced to ask the men to separate. As a consequence, Edward Horton left the inn at about 9.30 p.m., leaving John still drinking.

Edward Horton shared his home in Lower Westbrook with his grandson, John's son, who was also called John. When Edward arrived home from the pub he went

Bradford-on-Avon, 1910. (Author's collection)

straight to bed, while his grandson stayed up until 11 p.m. before finally retiring for the night.

John Horton junior was awakened at around midnight by the sounds of shouting and tremendous crashing noises. It was a bright, moonlit night and through the open door of his bedroom, he could see Edward standing on the landing, shouting, while from downstairs came the unmistakeable sounds of crockery and furniture being smashed.

Without a thought for his grandfather's safety, eighteen-year-old John bolted into the back bedroom and hid under the bed. As he peered out from his hiding place, John clearly saw his father walk up the stairs and push his grandfather into the other bedroom.

Seeing the bedroom door slam shut behind the two men, young John seized his chance and ran to neighbours for assistance. He returned minutes later with two men, Mr Hobbs and Mr Preedy and, as he approached his grandfather's cottage, he saw his father run out of the house and disappear into the night.

The scene in the cottage was one of utter devastation, a mess of broken crockery and furniture, which had, in the words of a contemporary newspaper, been 'smashed to atoms'. In the midst of it all lay Edward Horton, bruised and bleeding, with one of his legs very obviously badly broken.

A doctor was called and the compound fracture was set. However, a closer examination of Edward Horton revealed that he also had many other wounds. The old man had numerous cuts and bruises on his legs and arms and a sizeable chunk of flesh had been completely removed from his left wrist. By the following morning, his throat was hugely swollen and it became apparent that the left side of his chest appeared to have been completely crushed. Edward's injuries were very much worse than first thought and the old man was to die later that day. A post-mortem examination, conducted by Dr Highmore, showed that Edward had several broken ribs and the cause of his death was attributed to the crushing in of his ribs and to shock.

When John Horton left his father's house in the dead of night, he did not return to his home but instead went to seek out Charlotte Lindsey, banging on the door of her house and demanding to be let in. When he was refused entry, he picked up a large stone and used it to break the door down and, when he finally got inside the house and confronted Charlotte, he proceeded to beat her almost to death.

John Horton went to work as normal on Saturday, the day after he had violently attacked both his father and Charlotte. Once there, he had a conversation with a colleague, John Mead, that amounted almost to a confession to his involvement in both attacks. Mead told Horton that he had heard that he had been to Tory and beaten Charlotte Lindsey. 'Our old man got it worse than she,' replied Horton. Mead told him that it is was 'a thousand pities' if he had anything to do with it and that he expected the police would be arriving soon. 'I expect so too,' said Horton, going on to say that he didn't expect to go to prison when the police heard both sides of the argument. 'It might cost me £10 to get out of it,' he told Mead, before shrugging his shoulders and saying philosophically, 'It's done now and I shall have to put up with it.'

When the police called at his home to question him he was still at work but his daughter, Caroline, was at home and she told the police that when her father had returned home in the early hours of that morning, he had demanded a clean shirt as the one he was wearing was bloodied around the cuffs. Horton was apprehended when he returned home from work by PC Alfred Bailey, who promptly arrested him and charged him with the attack on Charlotte Lindsey. 'Ain't I also charged with assaulting my father as well?' asked Horton.

'Not at present,' replied Bailey.

'Because I gave both of them a damned good hiding and, if I had done my duty, I should have done for the pair of them, I was so provoked,' said Horton. Horton was asked the whereabouts of the stick that he had been seen carrying in the pub at Bradford on 20 November. 'I'm not bound to tell,' replied Horton. 'If I am to be charged with assaulting my father, I shall keep things dark.' At the police station, he was informed that his father was dead. 'Then I shall swing for that,' was Horton's only response.

By now, there were serious concerns that Charlotte Lindsey would not survive the brutal beating she had received and it was thought prudent to take her deposition. Horton was allowed to be present and heard Charlotte naming him as her assailant. The timing of the deposition proved fortuitous as Charlotte died from her injuries on the Monday after she had been attacked.

Horton's home had been thoroughly searched on the Sunday and a mattock was found hidden behind some garden tools and a loose board in an outhouse. As well as being covered in blood, the mattock bore traces of human hair and tiny fragments of glass. The mattock was shown to Horton at the police station and he was asked if he knew anything about it. Having examined it closely, Horton said, 'That is my old hoe. Where did you get it from?' When he was told where it had been found he insisted that that was not its proper place. 'But I could never have used that on my old father, could I?' he asked, adding, 'Then I may. I don't know.' He was also asked to account for the blood on his shirt cuffs, which he explained away by saying that he had cut himself shaving.

John Horton was charged with the wilful murder of both his father and Charlotte Lindsey. His trial opened at Devizes on 12 January 1886 before Mr Justice Groves, with Mr Murch and Mr Lopes prosecuting and Mr Charles Mathews defending. The proceedings got off to a bad start as, when the trial began at ten o'clock, it was immediately discovered that vital witnesses for the prosecution had not yet arrived. The judge was forced to delay proceedings to await the arrival of the 10.08 a.m. train from Bradford, which, in the event, was actually twelve minutes late. By the time the witnesses arrived at 10.30 a.m., the judge was furious, insisting that if they couldn't have stayed overnight in Devizes then the least they could have done was caught an earlier train.

There had been some questions about the legality of the declaration made by Charlotte Lindsey, hence it was decided that her case should be held in abeyance and Horton was tried only for the murder of his father, to which charge he pleaded 'Not guilty.'

Mr Murch, for the prosecution, related the events on 20 November and called several witnesses, including Samuel Hobbs, the neighbour who had gone to John Horton junior's assistance, the landlord of the Three Horse Shoes, Dr Highmore and the investigating officers. However, his chief witnesses were Caroline and John Horton junior, the defendant's own children.

Once all the evidence had been heard it was left to Mr Mathews to address the jury on behalf of the defence. Having called no witnesses, he immediately admitted that John Horton had been at his father's home on the evening of 20 November, but cautioned the jury against drawing any conclusions from that admission. The onus was on the prosecution to prove that, not only was the prisoner there at the time, but that he was there with the intention of taking his father's life. There was no way of knowing exactly what occurred at the house, said Mathews. What was done by the prisoner and what was done by the deceased man himself was a matter of great uncertainty and Mathews cautioned the jury that they would be taking a great leap in the dark – and taking that leap with awful consequences – if they returned a verdict of guilty of wilful murder against the defendant.

The motive put forward by the prosecution, Mathews continued, was that the crime was inspired by jealousy. 'Jealousy of what?' asked Mathews, somewhat scornfully. There was no evidence to support the notion that Charlotte Lindsey was the cause of any jealousy between Horton and his father and, without such evidence, there was no suggestion of a motive.

Mathews then went on to describe John Horton's previous good character, describing him as a good father, a good workman and a good friend. Horton had paid the rent on his father's home, suggesting that there was a normal and friendly father and son relationship between them. He urged them to believe his client, who had categorically stated, 'I intended no harm to my old father.'

He reminded the jury that although John Horton junior was adamant that he had seen his father entering his grandfather's room that night, he was unable to recall whether or not his father had anything in his hands at the time. If there had been an implement or weapon of any kind in John Horton senior's hands, said Mathews, then his son would have seen it and there was an excellent reason why he hadn't seen it – it wasn't there.

After John junior had run from the house to seek assistance, nobody but Edward

and John Horton knew what happened. The jury might draw inferences conclusive to their own minds but these would be merely inferences and a matter of pure speculation on their part.

Did Edward Horton go downstairs? If he went downstairs and found his son smashing up his furniture, did he then interfere to try and stop him? Mathews told the jury that he could not justify any violence by the prisoner but if John Horton had become engaged in a scuffle with his father, his blood being up, he might have grabbed the old man's throat and thrown him down. He reminded the court that Dr Highmore had stated that it was not impossible that Edward's injuries could have been incurred as a result of him falling downstairs.

Horton, by his own admission, had gone to his father's house with the intention of wrecking the furniture so that the old man would be unable to make a home with 'that old whore' Charlotte Lindsey. There simply wasn't sufficient evidence to show that John Horton had engaged in a deadly encounter. It was equally possible that Edward Horton, who was elderly and disabled, had engaged in a struggle with his son and tried to get back upstairs and, in doing so, fell down and sustained the injuries that ultimately caused his death. With that in mind, the jury would be quite justified in returning a verdict of guilty of manslaughter rather than guilty of murder.

The jury listened to the judge's summary of the case before retiring to consider their verdict. They returned after eighteen minutes and announced that they had found the prisoner 'Guilty of wilful murder'.

The judge put on his black cap and addressed the prisoner. He told him that he sincerely believed that the jury had reached the only possible conclusion open to them from the evidence that they had heard. Referring to the murder of Charlotte Lindsey, the judge stressed that he was unable to comment on any case that was not before him at this moment. However, he pointed out that Horton had acted in a perfectly reckless, wild state of passion, possibly fuelled by drink and had cruelly battered an old man who, until woken by his son, was in all probability in a state of perfect sleep in his own dwelling house.

Horton remained unmoved by the judge's speech and by the pronunciation of the death sentence that followed it. However, as he was leaving the dock, he muttered something unintelligible – only those who were closest to him at the time heard him complain that some of the witnesses had not spoken the truth.

His protest was to no avail as he was hanged by James Berry at Devizes on 1 February 1886. Since Horton had been convicted of patricide, there was nothing to gain from trying him for the murder of Charlotte Lindsey, although the indictment against him for her murder remained on file and the case was considered solved.

[Note: On occasions, Charlotte Lindsey's surname is alternatively spelled Lindsay.]

14

'WHAT WAS THE DISPUTE AS TO THE CHILD ABOUT?'

Devizes, 1889

After serving in the Army for eighteen years, Benjamin Purnell left the services and obtained a job as a porter in the Devizes Union Workhouse. It was there that he met and married his wife, Emily, although theirs was definitely not a match made in heaven. Emily was said to be 'of a very aggravating disposition', while Benjamin possessed a hair-trigger temper; the two fought like cat and dog. Within months of their marriage they had decided to live apart. Emily moved in with her brother, Edward Hampton, acting as housekeeper at his cottage in Avon Terrace, and Benjamin left the area. The couple's one child stayed with Emily.

In May 1889, nine years after their marriage, Benjamin unexpectedly arrived back in Devizes. He found himself a steady job as a stone breaker for the Rural Sanitary Authority and he and Emily decided to give their relationship a second chance. Accordingly, Benjamin moved into Edward Hampton's cottage. It was not a move that Hampton welcomed, as he was not at all fond of his brother-in-law. However, he did not feel that it was his place to keep a husband and wife apart and so grudgingly agreed to sharing his home. The cottage in Avon Terrace was only small and the Purnell's were forced to share a bedroom with one of their nephews, Caleb.

Benjamin and Emily quickly fell back into their old ways of arguing about anything and everything and Benjamin was often heard to threaten to 'do for' his wife. In the early morning hours of 9 November 1889, he finally made good his threats.

On the previous day, Emily had treated herself to a new flannel petticoat. This simple act infuriated Benjamin, who accused her of wasting money. A furious row ensued and, when the couple eventually retired to bed, they were not on speaking terms.

Market Square, Devizes, in the 1950s. (Author's collection)

At just before 6 a.m. on 9 November, Edward Hampton left the house as usual to go to his work as a snuff curer. He noticed a light burning in his sister and brother-in-law's bedroom, but neither heard nor saw any other signs to indicate that the couple were not sleeping peacefully. Shortly afterwards, Caleb Hampton was awakened by his uncle Benjamin getting out of bed. Benjamin picked up the new petticoat, which was hanging on the bedpost and walked out of the room with it, grumbling unintelligibly to himself as he did.

Shortly afterwards, Emily also got up and began to get dressed. She was most put out when she couldn't find her petticoat and, dressed only in her chemise, picked up the lamp from the room and followed her husband downstairs.

Caleb and his two brothers, who shared a bedroom with their father, clearly heard the previous night's argument start afresh. 'Give me my petticoat!' demanded Emily, to which her husband replied angrily, 'Go along, or I will break your skull.'

Things went ominously quiet downstairs for four or five minutes then all three boys heard a series of heavy thumping sounds, followed by silence. The three boys crept downstairs to see what was happening. Their uncle was standing in the front room in his shirtsleeves, taking a waistcoat and coat out of a drawer to finish getting dressed. One of the boys asked Benjamin where his aunt was, but got no reply.

Since Emily was nowhere to be seen, the boy opened the back door and looked outside. He immediately spotted a strange shape in a corner at the far end of the yard, about 7yds from the door and, as he got closer, he realised that it was his aunt Emily who was lying on her back unconscious, the lamp still tucked under her arm.

Sending his younger brother to find a policeman, the boy roused Mr Hillier, the next-door neighbour, who immediately sent for a doctor. When Dr Cowrie arrived just minutes later he quickly organised a stretcher and had Emily conveyed to the cottage hospital at Devizes, where she was admitted to the woman's ward. Only then did anyone take a close look at her injuries, which were so severe that it was quite evident that Emily Purnell stood absolutely no chance of surviving. She died at five o'clock on the following morning, without ever having regained consciousness and a later post-mortem examination noted the presence of six serious wounds to her head, five of which had actually fractured her skull. Any one of the five fractures would have been sufficient to cause her death. A heavy hatchet, bearing traces of blood and human hair, was found in the yard a few feet from where her body had been lying, along with the remnants of her new petticoat, which had been torn to shreds.

The police were at Avon Terrace within minutes of the attack on Emily Purnell. PC Selman had been close by, patrolling his beat near to the railway station, but in spite of the speed of his arrival, when he got there Benjamin Purnell had disappeared. It was later established that, having finished getting dressed, he had walked into Devizes and gone to the borough police station, with the intention of giving himself up. Finding nobody there, he began to walk to the county police station, near to where he was arrested by Superintendent Baldwin later that morning. When first questioned by the police, Purnell told them, 'I know I beat my wife' and, when informed the next morning that Emily was dead, his only reaction was to say, 'Oh, is she?'

An inquest was held into the death of Emily Purnell, presided over by coroner Mr F.T. Sylvester. It was surmised that Emily had either been told by Benjamin or had merely suspected that her new petticoat was in the yard and had gone outside to look for it by the light of the petroleum lamp that she had carried downstairs from the bedroom. It was evident that Emily had not been attacked inside the house since the severity of her injuries meant that she would almost certainly have dropped to the ground as soon as she was first struck. Had she run out of the house to escape her husband's violence, it was unlikely that she would have taken the lamp with her, and, in all probability, she would have screamed or cried out. Since no screams had been heard, the inquest determined that the most likely scenario was that forty-four-year-old Emily was attacked as she bent to gather up the scraps of her ruined petticoat. The coroner's jury returned a verdict of wilful murder against Benjamin Purnell, who was committed for trial at the next Wiltshire Assizes.

Shortly before his trial opened at Devizes, Purnell sent in an application to the judge, Baron Pollock, to be assigned a defence counsel since he was unable to afford to hire one. His request was granted and Mr Hussey Walsh was appointed to defend him, while Mr F.R.Y. Radcliffe and Mr Lopes prosecuted.

When the charge of wilful murder was read out to him at the opening of the proceedings, a haggard looking Purnell promptly pleaded 'Guilty'. The court clerk approached him and asked him directly if he was pleading guilty or not guilty. 'Yes, I am guilty of the charge,' responded Purnell. It was only after a brief consultation with his counsel that Purnell changed his plea to the more customary 'Not Guilty' and the trial began.

Mr Radcliffe told the court of the Purnell's unhappy marriage and of the constant bickering between him and his wife, before relating the events of the morning of 9 November. After hearing from several material witnesses, it was then left to Mr Hussey Walsh to present the case for the defence.

The defence counsel mysteriously told the court that there were circumstances in the case that had not been disclosed by the evidence and which he himself was unable to divulge. He did drop a very subtle hint to the jury, saying that it might give them cause for reflection. He had questioned Mr Hampton's children and had asked each of them the question, 'What was the dispute as to the child about?' All of the children had agreed that the argument between Benjamin and Emily Purnell that had preceded her murder was about 'the child', although none of the children seemed to know why the couple should be quarrelling. Mr Hussey Walsh told the jury that there were many suppositions open to them, but he would leave them to wonder why there was so much mystery surrounding the cause of the argument.

The case for the prosecution was straightforward, according to prosecuting counsel, Mr Radcliffe. The number of blows struck and the choice of weapon proved conclusively that Benjamin Purnell had intended to murder his wife – after all, anybody who picked up a large hatchet and struck someone on the head with it six times must surely realise that they were likely to kill that person. Counsel for the defence disagreed. Mr Hussey Walsh put it to the jury that there had been dire provocation by the victim and that her husband had snatched the first weapon to hand and struck her in hot blood, without any intention of killing her.

The jury chose to believe the prosecution's version of events, finding fifty-one-year-old Benjamin Purnell guilty of the wilful murder of his wife, Emily. Purnell listened to Baron Pollock's sentence of death with a dazed, somewhat despairing look on his face before being taken from the court back to prison at Devizes, where hangman James Berry carried out the sentence on 9 December 1889. Afterwards, Purnell's body was buried within the prison walls.

The defence counsel's enigmatic hints about an argument concerning a child remain a tantalising mystery. However, in reporting the murder, the local newspapers of the time clearly state that Benjamin and Emily Purnell had one child, who lived with Emily at her brother's home. Yet curiously, in describing the sleeping arrangements at Avon Terrace, the same newspapers also state that the cottage had two bedrooms, one occupied by Emily's brother, Mr Hampton and two of his sons, the other by Emily, Benjamin and Caleb, the youngest son of Mr Hampton. No mention is made of the whereabouts of the Purnell's child, who, assuming that he or she was born in wedlock, would have been eight or nine years old at the time of Emily's murder – the same age as Caleb Hampton. A search of the records pertaining to the Hampton family seem to indicate that, by the time Caleb was one month old, his father, Edward, is recorded as being widowed.

Were the contemporary newspapers simply mistaken in reporting that the Purnell's had a child together and that this child lived with Emily at Avon Terrace? If not, where was he or she when the murder occurred? Was this 'the child' referred to by the counsel for the defence during the trial? And, if so, why was he or she the subject of the argument that precipitated Emily's murder? Why was Mr Hussey Walsh unable to reveal any further details, particularly if these details might possibly have saved his client's life? Was Emily Purnell really killed simply because she had frittered her money away on a new petticoat or was there another motive? So long after the murder, it seems that these questions are destined to remain unanswered.

[Note: Some recently written accounts of the murder, particularly those on the internet, give the couple's name as Purcell and the location of the murder as Bradford-upon-Avon. In writing this account, I have taken information from contemporary newspapers, which use the name Purnell and give the location of the murder as Devizes. (Hampton's residence is confirmed as Avon Court, Devizes in census records of the time.)]

15

'DO YOU WANT ME, SIR?'

John Gurd was born in 1861, one of four children of a master shoemaker from Donhead St Mary, near Shaftesbury. Sadly, Gurd's father died when John was five years old, leaving his mother to bring up her family alone on whatever money she could earn as a dressmaker.

John grew up and joined the Army, serving first in the Dorset Militia then transferring to the Dorset Regiment. For reasons unknown, he then enlisted in the Royal Marines under the alias Louis Hamilton. However, by 1890, he had contracted an illness that was sufficiently severe for him to be invalided out of the Marines with a pension. Still under his assumed name, he applied for a job as an attendant at the Wiltshire County Asylum in Devizes

There he met and courted a pretty under housemaid, Florence Adams. The couple became engaged, but, in 1892, with only a week to go before their wedding, Florence found out that her husband-to-be owed money to several patients at the asylum and also to local tradesmen. The amount was only £3, but Florence had no wish to start her married life in debt and wrote to John Gurd calling off their nuptials.

Gurd was furious. He immediately wrote back to Florence threatening to kill her if she ever married another man, but Florence did not take his threats seriously. Gurd brooded about his broken engagement and came to the erroneous conclusion that Florence's uncle, Henry Richards, was to blame. Richards had never hidden his dislike of his niece's fiancé and had been against the marriage from the word go.

No doubt wishing to distance himself from his former fiancée, Gurd handed in his notice at the asylum and returned to his family in Shaftesbury. Yet resentment and anger continued to build up inside him and, on 8 April 1892, he travelled back to Melksham, determined to seek out Henry Richards and confront him about his part in persuading his niece to call off the wedding.

Gurd walked around Melksham for several hours looking for Richards, finally locating him in a public house. Becoming increasingly angry and vengeful by

Spa Road, Melksham, 1915. (Author's collection)

the minute, Gurd waited outside the pub until Richards left the premises then, as Richards was walking home along Spa Road, Gurd pulled a revolver from his coat pocket and shot Richards twice in the back. As Richards fell to the ground mortally wounded, his assassin simply turned and walked away.

Unfortunately for Gurd, the incident had been witnessed by a woman who was subsequently able to give police an excellent description of the killer. Another bystander, Mr Harris, actually asked Gurd what the noise was, to be told that it was only some boys letting off firecrackers.

The police immediately issued a description of 'Louis Hamilton', which stated that he was wanted for wilful murder at Melksham. He was described as 'aged 29, height 5ft 7in, with a fair complexion, sandy moustache, no whiskers, with a thin face and dark brown hair, rather curly or frizzy.' The description also carried a warning: 'May be carrying a revolver'. A massive hunt for the fugitive was launched, with police following up supposed sightings of Gurd in Bath and Frome.

On 12 April, the landlord of the White Hart Inn at Corsley was holding a 'lock in', with several of his customers enjoying an after-hours drink. They were disturbed by a loud banging on the door of the pub, which the landlord went to answer. He was confronted by Gurd, demanding entry. After spending three days on the run, Gurd's appearance gave him the look of a down and out and the landlord told him in no uncertain terms to leave the premises, slamming the door in his face. Moments later, the drinkers heard the sound of a gunshot from outside the pub and, when they went to investigate, they saw the dishevelled Gurd disappearing in the direction of Melksham. One of the drinker's horses, which had been tethered in the pub yard, had been shot in the neck.

The police were summoned and, after questioning the landlord and getting his description, determined that the man who had confronted him on the pub doorstep

Spa Road, Melksham, 2008. (© N. Sly)

was their fugitive. Four uniformed policemen – Superintendent Perrett, Sergeant Molden and two constables – quickly set off along the Frome road in pursuit of their quarry.

They caught up with him about 300yds from the gates of Longleat Park. Hearing their approach Gurd called out, 'Do you want me, Sir?'

'I believe I do,' replied Superintendent Perrett.

At that, Gurd turned and ran back towards the police officers, reaching into his coat pocket as he ran. Perrett guessed that the man was about to pull out a gun and managed to seize Gurd around the waist and throw him to the ground. As they fell, two shots rang out and Sergeant Molden immediately cried out, 'Oh dear! I'm shot!'

The other officers grappled with Gurd and Constable Langley finally managed to seize his gun and disarm him. Only when Gurd was subdued were the officers able to attend to their fallen colleague, who was lying in the road, clutching his side with one hand. He was taken to a nearby cottage, but before medical assistance could arrive, he uttered his last words, 'Lord have mercy on my soul', and died. It was later found that one bullet from Gurd's gun had entered his left breast.

Gurd, now safely handcuffed, was asked why he shot the sergeant and replied, 'Because you didn't give me time to shoot myself.'

Sergeant Enos Molden was buried at Christ Church, Warminster with full police honours. His funeral was attended by more than 120 of his fellow officers, including the chief constable. Tragically, he had been due to retire to the village of Shrewton on the day after his death. Having served for eleven years, villagers had planned to celebrate his return with a testimonial and a marble clock, specially purchased for the occasion.

The High Street, Melksham, in the 1960s. (Author's collection)

Gurd appeared before the Melksham magistrates on 20 April, charged with the murders of Henry Richards and Sergeant Enos Molden. He was committed for trial at the next Wiltshire Assizes at Salisbury.

When the trial opened before Mr Justice Charles, Gurd shocked everybody by pleading guilty. Mr Charles told him that he must stand his trial but Gurd insisted , 'I wish to say I am guilty and I am quite willing to pay for what I have done.'

Eventually, he was persuaded to plead not guilty and his defence counsel tried to convince the jury that Gurd had been very depressed at the time of the shootings as a result of the end of his engagement and that, on both occasions, he had been drinking heavily before committing the murders. However, the jury had already heard Gurd's confession at the beginning of the trial and thus any attempt at defending him was futile. They took just eight minutes at the end of the trial to return with a verdict of 'Guilty' and Gurd was promptly sentenced to death.

James Billington carried out his execution at Devizes on 26 July 1892. Billington made a slight error in calculating the necessary drop and, as a result, Gurd's death was due to shock rather than dislocation of the spinal vertebrae. Even so, it was recorded as having been 'practically instantaneous'. Before his death, Gurd had expressed remorse at killing Sergeant Molden, but had shown no contrition for the murder of Henry Richards and, indeed, had spoken of his intentions to kill Florence Adams at the same time as he had murdered her uncle. Had she been out with her uncle on the evening of his murder, as she often was, Gurd would undoubtedly have shot her too.

16

'THE CURSE OF MY LIFE'

Swindon, 1903

The banns for the marriage of Edward Richard Palmer and Esther Swinford had been posted, but the wedding never took place. The exact reasons why the marriage didn't happen depended on whether you were to ask Edward or Esther. Edward maintained that somebody had told him something very revealing about his fiancée and, as a consequence, he just couldn't bring himself to marry her. Meanwhile Esther gave a completely different account; according to her, Edward was untrustworthy. She had given him a considerable sum of money, with which to find and furnish their future marital home, and he had frittered it all away on other things, mainly drink.

Regardless of why their nuptials didn't happen, Edward left Swindon, where the couple had planned to start their married life, and moved away. He obtained work as a gardener for a Mr Lacey near Reading, then a Captain Pirie at Marlow. It was at about this time that he began to carry a revolver. His brother was so concerned by this that he confiscated the weapon, but Edward pleaded with him to give it back, saying that he was frightened of being left alone at work. His brother finally relented and returned the gun in the summer of 1903.

Esther continued to work as a barmaid at the Ship Inn in Swindon. Even though she and Edward had broken off their engagement, there were still vestiges of warmth and attraction between them and they continued to write affectionately to each other.

In early September 1903, Edward applied to return to his former job as a labourer with the GWR Works at Swindon, although his application was ultimately unsuccessful. He made up his mind that, without work, there was no future for him in Swindon, so decided to try his luck at Newbury. On the point of leaving the area again, he wanted to see Esther to say goodbye, so on 18 September he visited the Ship Inn, deliberately choosing a time when he knew that the pub would be deserted.

Esther served Palmer with a bottle of Bass beer and the two remained alone in the bar for a few moments. Suddenly, the landlord and landlady, who were

The GWR Works, Swindon, 1928. (Author's collection)

in their private quarters at the rear of the pub, heard the sound of a gunshot. They immediately rushed to the bar, where they found Esther lying on the floor, obviously dying, with Edward standing gazing wistfully at her, the gun still in his hand.

The landlord announced that he was going to send for the police, at which Palmer turned to him and said sadly; 'You needn't do that, Walt, I done it. I loved the girl.' As they waited for the police and a doctor, twenty-year-old Esther Swinford died from a single bullet wound to the heart.

When the police arrived, Edward Palmer went with them without protest and made no reply when he was formally charged with Esther's wilful murder. When he was searched at the police station a photograph of Esther was found in his pocket, on which he had written the words 'The curse of my life'.

At the inquest into the death of Esther Swinford, the jury returned a verdict of wilful murder against Edward Palmer, who was committed to stand trial at the next Wiltshire Assizes. His trial opened at Devizes on 28 October 1903, before Mr Justice Wills. Mr J.A. Foote KC and Mr Seton acted for the prosecution and Mr Thornton Lawes defended.

The prosecution began by outlining the circumstances under which Esther and Edward had broken off their engagement, dismissing the idea that Palmer had heard anything untoward about Esther and pointing to the letters between the couple as evidence that Palmer had spent the money that he should have used to secure accommodation for them after their marriage. The court was told that Edward's brother had been so concerned about Palmer that he had forcibly taken his gun from him, only returning it reluctantly because he believed that his brother was truly afraid of being set upon and attacked.

Esther Swinford. (Courtesy of John Broderick)

Mr Foote maintained that Palmer had deliberately chosen to visit the Ship Inn at a time when he knew that he was almost certain to be alone with Esther and that he had taken his loaded gun with him with the express purpose of shooting her.

Edward Palmer took the stand in his own defence. He maintained that he had habitually carried a loaded revolver for about nine years and admitted that he had taken it with him when he went to see Esther on the evening of 18 September. According to Palmer, Esther had behaved very coolly towards him. He had asked her for a smoke to accompany his beer and she picked up a box of cigars and opened the lid, holding the box out for Edward to take one.

He had tried to take her hand as she did so, saying, 'Hettie, won't you wish me goodbye as I am going away tomorrow?' Esther replied, 'I do not wish to have any more to do with you,' and, at this, Palmer told the court that he had pulled out his gun and pointed it at her, with the aim of frightening her into speaking to him. Esther dropped the box of cigars that she was proffering and grabbed Palmer's wrist with both hands. Her tight grip had caused the gun to go off accidentally and Esther had immediately fallen to the ground, mortally wounded.

Palmer admitted to writing the words 'The curse of my life' on his photograph of Esther, but declined to divulge why he had done so and was unable or unwilling to provide any instances of how Esther might have wronged him.

Since Palmer had been found standing over the body of his victim with the literal 'smoking gun' in his hand, the defence team had an uphill struggle to try and save him from execution. They called several witnesses to testify to his previous good character, including all of his former employers who, without exception, described him as a steady, hard-working young man. A doctor had already appeared for the prosecution to say that, in his opinion, Palmer's mental state was quite normal, both now and at the time of the murder. Hence the defence chose to concentrate on demonstrating that Palmer's previous good character negated any question of malice aforethought and that, in grabbing Edward's wrists, Esther had precipitated the firing of the gun and accidentally brought about her own demise. It was therefore the contention of the defence that the charge should be reduced from murder to manslaughter.

The jury did not agree with the defence team. After a short debate, they returned a verdict of 'Guilty of wilful murder' against twenty-four-year-old Edward Richard Palmer, who was promptly sentenced to death by Mr Justice Wills.

William Billington carried out the execution at Devizes on 17 November 1903, assisted by his brother, John. (The two Billington brothers were part of a family dynasty of British hangmen as their father, James, and their older brother, Thomas, had both previously held the post of official hangman.) Unwittingly, and through no fault of her own, Esther Swinford had indeed become the curse of Palmer's life.

17

'I HAVE TOLD YOU THE TRUTH. HE IS WHERE I HAVE TAKEN HIM TO'

Burbage, 1907

On 23 April 1908, farm labourer William Fidler and his colleague were taking a welcome break from their work to eat their lunch when they made a chilling discovery that must surely have ruined their appetites. In a disused well in a field on Southgrove Farm, near Burbage, they found the badly decomposed body of a young boy.

An inquest into the death of the so far unidentified child was opened at the White Hart Inn in Burbage where the local doctor, Dr Farquhar, gave evidence that the boy was about twelve years old and, in his opinion, had been in the well for about nine months. No missing children had been reported in the area during the time the boy's body had lain undiscovered in the well, but gypsies often used the field in which the well was situated as a camp and it was believed that the dead child might have come from a gypsy family. With no clues to the boy's identity and with his body showing no obvious marks of violence and being too decomposed to provide sufficient evidence as to the cause of his death, the inquest recorded an open verdict.

It was almost three years before a possible identity was suggested for the child, who had since been interred in Burbage churchyard, his death recorded as that of an 'unknown boy'. Mary Ann Nash had given birth to an illegitimate son on 16 September 1901 and named him Stanley George Nash. Having a baby meant the end of Mary Ann's freedom and she soon arranged for him to lodge with her father at his home in Milkhouse Water, Pewsey Vale, with Mary Ann contributing to her son's upkeep. When she defaulted on her agreed payments, the child's grandfather wrote and told her that he could not afford to keep the boy and Mary Ann was forced to make other arrangements for her son's care. She agreed terms with Mrs Mary Jane Stagg to keep her son, while she continued to work in London. However, in May 1907, while Mary Ann was between jobs and staying with her aunt and uncle at

Burbage at the turn of the century. (Author's collection)

their home in Collingbourne Kingston, Mrs Stagg turned up on her doorstep with Stanley in tow. Once again Mary Ann had failed to keep up with the agreed payments for her child's care and his foster mother could no longer keep him if his mother was unwilling to pay for his keep.

Mary Ann's aunt and uncle, Emma and Ephraim Stagg, flatly refused to board the child for their niece, insisting that she took him to the workhouse. Thus Stanley lived in the workhouse until 27 June 1907, when his mother came to collect him, saying that she had made new arrangements for his care with an old school friend, a woman named Mrs Hillier who lived in Crabtree Cottages, Savernake Forest. Stanley was dressed in his Sunday best suit, with a jaunty sailor cap and lace-up boots and taken to meet his new guardian. Later that day, Mary Ann arrived back at her aunt and uncle's home alone. She told her aunt and uncle that she had safely delivered Stanley to Mrs Hillier, who had tucked him up in bed with her own children. A few days later, she had packed up all Stanley's clothes and announced her intention of taking the parcel to Mrs Hillier.

Stanley was never seen again, although whenever Mary Ann was asked about him, she always told people that he was doing well, even stating that he had been on a holiday to Reading. It took until 1911 for someone to realise that Stanley was missing and to connect this information with the discovery of the body of the unidentified male child in Burbage. Police questioned Mary Ann Nash, who repeated her story that the boy was lodging at Savernake Forest. Mrs Stagg pointed out that the police were sure to check with Mrs Hillier, but Mary Ann was insistent, telling her aunt, 'I have told you the truth. He is where I have taken him to.'

Naturally, the police went straight to interview Mrs Hillier who admitted to knowing Mary Ann but denied ever having been placed in charge of Stanley.

When Mary Ann Nash was unable to provide the police with a true account of her son's current whereabouts, she was arrested by Inspector Elkins and charged with his wilful murder.

Mary Ann Nash appeared before a special sitting of magistrates at Marlborough on 27 March 1911. On 14 March, the child had been exhumed from his grave in Burbage and his almost skeletonised body examined by Mr Pepper of the Home Office. Pepper determined that the child was considerably younger than had first been thought, putting his age at between five and seven years old. He based his conclusions on an examination of the boy's teeth, noting that the boy had only one permanent molar on each side of his upper and lower jaws, the remaining teeth being milk teeth. Pepper also found that the body had very light brown, almost yellow hair, as had Stanley Nash.

Mary Ann Nash was committed for trial at the next Wiltshire Assizes for the wilful murder of her son. Her trial opened on 31 May 1911 at Salisbury, before Mr Justice Coleridge. Mr F.R.Y. Radcliffe and Mr Emmanuel appeared for the prosecution, while Mr Rayner Goddard defended Mary Ann, who pleaded 'Not Guilty' to the charge against her.

By the start of the trial, further investigations had been carried out on the remains of Stanley Nash, who would have been five years and nine months old at the time of his death. Dr W.H. Dolamore of the Royal Dental Hospital in London had examined his skull and concurred with Mr Pepper and Dr Oliver Maurice, the police surgeon from Marlborough. All agreed that the child was about six years old, give or take three or four months. The dead child's clothes had been examined and, although badly rotted through having been in water for so long, were found to resemble those that Stanley was wearing when he was last seen alive, leaving the workhouse. In particular, the child had been found with a hatband around his forehead and Pepper had been able to discern the name of a ship, HMS *Swift*, painted on it in gold letters.

While the prosecution maintained that Mary Ann Nash had killed her son by putting the boy into the well, the defence insisted that there was no case to answer. Mr Goddard pointed out that the body of the unknown boy had never been formally identified as being that of Stanley Nash and that there was no evidence that the child had been murdered. Even if there were, there was absolutely no evidence to suggest that it was Mary Ann Nash who had killed her boy – Stanley could have been murdered by almost anyone.

Goddard failed to convince the jury with his arguments and they retired for just eight minutes before returning with a verdict of 'Guilty', albeit with a recommendation of mercy for the accused. In passing sentence of death, Mr Justice Coleridge told Mary Ann Nash that she had put her son to a dreadful death and that the mind shuddered at her total absence of all feelings of maternity and humanity.

With Stanley Nash dead and his mother sentenced to death for his murder, the 'Wiltshire Well Mystery', as it was referred to in the newspapers of the day, had been responsible for yet another controversy. Dr Farquhar, who had originally told the inquest in 1908 that the unidentified remains were those of a twelve-year-old boy, was tried for perjury, having given false evidence in his examination before the magistrates, which might have prevented the correct identification of the child's body. Dr Farquhar had insisted that he had examined the child's teeth when the body was found and that he had told the police that the child was aged between nine and thirteen years. Yet Farquhar's description of the child's teeth did not coincide with that of the two expert witnesses at the trial. Claiming to have mislaid his notebook, in which he had recorded details of the case at the time of the discovery of the body, Farquhar subsequently managed to produce the book in court and his notes were found to substantiate his original evidence. However, the notebook had been heavily mutilated to remove pre-printed information and, on closer examination, was found to have been one issued as a free gift to doctors by Messrs Oppenheimer and Co., a firm of Wholesale Chemists from London. The notebook that Farquhar produced, claiming it to contain his original notes from 1908, could not possibly have been issued before 1911, since it referred to a drug, wychodine, which had not been marketed in 1908 and had not appeared in the printed diary in the position in which it appeared in Farquhar's copy until 1911. Farquhar had been afraid that his carelessness in losing his notes would affect his professional reputation and had lied under oath. He was committed for trial at the Wiltshire Assizes charged with 'falsely, wickedly, absolutely and corruptly committing wilful and corrupt perjury.'

Farquhar was eventually found guilty at his trial, but he was by now an old man and his career was ruined. The judge determined that the doctor's perjury had not adversely affected the court case against Mary Ann Nash and dealt with the doctor leniently, binding him over for the sum of £50. The doctor returned to Burbage where the villagers gave him a hero's welcome, hanging banners and bunting in the street to mark his return. However Farquhar was a broken man. He resigned from the Pewsey Board of Guardians, citing old age and increasing infirmities, and by the end of June 1911 he had sold up his medical practice and left the village.

Meanwhile, Mary Ann Nash's defence team had been busy putting together an appeal on her behalf. They also wrote a letter to the local newspapers to quash rumours that she had murdered another child, stating that the child in question was alive and well and living at the Marlborough Union Workhouse.

The crux of the appeal was that the prosecution had not successfully proved that the child's body was that of Stanley George Nash. Secondly, they had failed to demonstrate that the child had been unlawfully killed and finally they had failed to produce any evidence that the child's murder was committed by the accused, Mary Ann Nash. Mr Rayner Goddard maintained that Nash may have abandoned the child or given him to the gypsies that were known to frequent the area. She might even have given him to Mrs Hillier, who may have subsequently killed him.

The appeal court ruled that sufficient evidence had been provided to positively identify the dead child as Stanley George Nash. It was not disputed that the boy had last been seen alive in the company of his mother, who had subsequently lied about his whereabouts and well being. The circumstances of the child's death meant that it had to have occurred either as a result of foul play or accident and that either scenario would have been within Mary Ann Nash's knowledge. Had the boy died by accident, it would have been in her interests to say so and yet she had continued to insist that her son was safe with Mrs Hillier and that she was in contact with him and receiving reports of his progress.

With the appeal dismissed, Mary Ann Nash's execution was scheduled for 6 July 1911. However, a petition with some 14,000 signatures – including those of some of the members of her trial jury – was sent to the Home Office and, on the day before she was scheduled to die, she was given a temporary respite pending further instructions from the Home Office. The then Home Secretary, Winston Churchill, eventually commuted her sentence to life imprisonment.

18

'STOP THAT MAN; HE HAS MURDERED MY TEDDY'

Salisbury, 1908

On 31 October 1908, twelve-year-old Edwin Richard Haskell of Meadow Road, Fisherton in Salisbury went to bed at about ten o'clock at night. Edwin was disabled, having only one leg, but, in spite of his physical handicap, he was a cheerful boy who managed to play football and do all of the things that most boys of his age could do, although with the aid of crutch. However, it was Edwin's dream to buy himself a cork leg and, to that end, he saved every penny of his pocket money. Neighbours had taken pity on the boy and had contributed heavily to the fund and Edwin had amassed more than £8, which he kept in a box in his bedroom.

With Edwin tucked up in bed, his mother Flora, a widow, seized the opportunity to slip out to the shop, leaving her son alone in the house. She was gone for only fifteen minutes and had just returned home when her nephew, Percy Noble, called at the house. When Percy knocked on the back door at about half-past ten, he heard a loud thumping noise then his aunt shout out, 'Stop that man; he has murdered my Teddy.' Percy immediately ran to the front of the house, where he met his aunt who had run through the house and out of the front door, screaming loudly.

Her frantic cries brought a number of her neighbours out of their houses, none of whom saw any signs of a fleeing stranger in the dark street. One neighbour, Walter Steer, ran off down the road in the direction in which Flora was pointing and, as he turned the corner into York Road, he spotted two men standing by a public house. He knew one of the men by sight and asked him if he knew his companion. When the man said no, Steer followed the stranger for some distance, but, since he could still hear Flora screaming hysterically, he eventually abandoned his pursuit and went back to help her. He rushed into the Haskell's house, seizing a lantern on his way and climbing the stairs. He found Edwin Haskell lying dead in his bed, his throat slashed from ear to ear and his bedclothes soaked in blood. Steer called out to ask someone to summon a doctor and the police.

When the police arrived, Flora Haskell told them that just as her nephew had knocked on the back door, she had heard a thumping noise coming from Edwin's room. Suddenly, a strange man ran downstairs and out through the front door, throwing a knife at her as he made his escape. Flora was able to describe the intruder as being between thirty and forty years old, 5ft 6in tall, clean-shaven and dressed in a dark suit and a collarless shirt. He wore a light cap and may have also had a light overcoat.

Having collected a bloodstained knife, which lay on the floor at the bottom of the stairs, the police immediately launched a search for the man using bloodhounds and borrowing bicycles from members of the public to enable them to search further afield. However, only two days later it became obvious that the intensive manhunt was being scaled down. The bloodhounds were sent back to their kennels at Shrewton and the borrowed bicycles were returned to their owners. Mark Richardson, the Chief Constable of Wiltshire, enigmatically announced to the press that their inquiries into the murder of Edwin Haskell were now being chiefly confined to the neighbourhood of the crime.

The boy's funeral took place on 4 November, his coffin followed by twelve of his classmates from the Fisherton elementary school, each carrying a posy of white flowers. Numerous local dignitaries sent wreaths including Lady Hulse, Lady Tennant and Sir Walter and Lady Palmer, the former Member of Parliament for Salisbury and his wife. Salisbury Football Club also sent a wreath and there was another with the message 'In ever-loving memory of darling little Teddy from his loving mother and grandma.' At half-past ten that evening, his 'loving mother', Flora Fanny Haskell, was arrested, charged with the wilful murder of her son.

Richardson himself made the arrest, accompanied by Superintendent Stephens of the Wiltshire County Police and Chief Inspector Dew of Scotland Yard, who had been called in immediately after the murder to assist the local force with their investigations. Flora Haskell, described in the contemporary newspapers as 'a frail woman', could only repeat the words 'No, no, no' on her arrest.

An inquest into Edwin's death was opened at the Council House, Salisbury under City Coroner Mr S. Buchanan Smith. The first person to give evidence was John Stanley Wyatt, an assistant at the Co-operative Society Stores in Salisbury. On the night of the murder, Wyatt had tried to deliver a parcel to Mrs Haskell's neighbour, but had found nobody at home. He had knocked at Flora Haskell's door at about twenty-five past ten and asked her to take in the parcel, which she agreed to do. According to Wyatt, Flora Haskell appeared calm and collected and there was nothing unusual about her appearance.

Gertrude Steer had visited Flora at about 9.45 p.m. to deliver a coat that she had made for her. She too noticed nothing abnormal. Gertrude's father, Walter, was the neighbour who had found Edwin dead in his bed. He told the inquest that, having heard Flora screaming, he had rushed outside and immediately run in the direction in which Flora was pointing and saying 'man round the corner'.

Having heard evidence from the investigating officers, the coroner's jury delivered a verdict of wilful murder against Flora Haskell and she was committed for trial at the next Wiltshire Assizes.

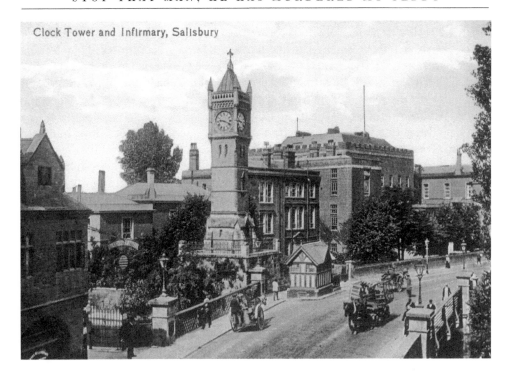

Clock Tower and Infirmary, Salisbury

Salisbury in the 1920s. (Author's collection)

Her trial opened at Devizes on 15 February 1909, presided over by Mr Justice Ridley. Mr Foote KC and Mr Parr prosecuted, while Mrs Haskell's defence was conducted by Mr Rayner Goddard and Mr Schuster.

One of the biggest issues of the case was the timing of the events of 31 October. It had now been established that delivery boy John Wyatt had actually seen Flora at 10.17 p.m. rather than, as first thought, at 10.25 p.m., when, according to him, she had been completely normal in both appearance and behaviour. The prosecution maintained that the murder had been committed between 10.25 p.m. and 10.30 p.m. Shortly afterwards, Percy Noble had come to the back door of the house and heard first a thump, then a scream. Flora Haskell's frantic shouts had sent him straight back to the street to summon help.

The kitchen sink was close to the back door and the prosecution suggested that Flora had had more than enough time to rinse the blood from her hands between first speaking to Noble and running screaming out of the front door shortly afterwards.

It was pointed out that after the intruder had run downstairs and left the house, throwing the knife at Flora on his way out, she had made no real attempt to either follow him herself, or even to go upstairs to check on her son. The first person to go up and see Edwin had been Walter Steer and that had been after he had followed the strange man for some time. In fact, nobody had checked to see if Edwin were alive or dead, although Flora had told several people that Teddy had been murdered by the time Steer had confirmed that fact. The bedroom in which Teddy was sleeping had appeared in perfect order, with nothing disturbed – with the obvious exception of the dead child lying in his blood-soaked bed.

The knife that had allegedly been thrown at Flora Haskell was a sharpened table knife, taken from her own kitchen. In addition, Flora had a great number of bloodstains on her blouse and skirt – far more than would have been expected from simply having a knife thrown at her. A bloody handkerchief had also been found in her pocket, although Flora insisted that Edwin had cut his head and the handkerchief had become stained when she had wiped the blood from the wound.

When the police arrived at her house after her son's murder, Flora had said nothing about her son's savings, only thinking to ask if they were still in his room at 3.30 a.m., some five hours after the murder. According to her, there should have been £8 2s in the tin where the money was kept, but police found only £3 10s. In her initial statements to the police, Flora had mentioned a man who, on the day before Edwin's death, had asked her for lodgings. It was also discovered that a Mr Mold had, on occasions, stayed with Flora at her home, although no suspicion of any involvement with Edwin's death was attached to him.

Percy Noble and his father, Alfred, told the court that Flora was always affectionate and loving towards Edwin, although Alfred did state that Flora had told him that she was contemplating marrying again.

The court next heard from a succession of residents of Meadow Road who had responded to Flora's hysterical screams. The first, dairyman Thomas Rawlings, also related that Flora had always appeared very fond of her son and seemed to be a good mother.

Emily Sweetman had noticed that Flora Haskell had a small scratch on her nose immediately after the murder, but was sure that it was not bleeding. On the following day, Emily had asked Flora if it had happened when the man threw the knife at her but had been told that Flora had caused the scratch herself with her ring.

William Golding, one of the first police officers on the scene, had sat on a chair outside the kitchen at Flora's house all night. While there, he had allowed Flora's mother, Mrs Carter, to sweep the floor of the kitchen and hallway and to wash the hall floor. Golding told the court that he had understood that this would be all right as long as nothing was done upstairs. 'I think it was a great piece of folly to do that,' remarked the judge.

The court then heard from medical witnesses. Dr Wilkes, the first doctor to attend, was at the scene within minutes of being called and was of the opinion that Edwin had been killed only about a quarter of an hour before his arrival. The boy's throat had been slashed and his windpipe cut, injuries that would, in Wilkes' opinion, have taken considerable force to inflict. Wilkes testified that Flora had leaned over and kissed Edwin after he had finished his examination of the boy, but stated that her clothes had not come into contact with any blood in the boy's bedroom.

Dr Rowe and Dr Kempe of Salisbury corroborated Wilkes' evidence. The final medical witness was Professor Pepper, an expert on bloodstains and adviser to the Home Office. Pepper had examined Flora's clothes and believed that the blood found on them could not result from a knife being thrown at her. He pointed out that some of the stains were elongated and were more likely to have been caused by blood dropping onto the clothes from some unidentified object or by a spray of blood projecting from a wound.

The last witness called was a police matron who told the court that, while in custody, Flora Haskell had said, 'If I did it, I do not remember it.'

Mr Foote, for the prosecution, simply stated that there was no doubt that the boy was murdered and that Flora Haskell and her son were alone in the house when the murder occurred. He reminded the court that nobody had seen anyone either at the house, leaving the house after the murder, or out in the street.

The defence counsel, Mr Goddard, having called no witnesses, then addressed the jury. The prisoner had always been most affectionate to her son and the crime, if done by her, must have been done on impulse. The prosecution, said Mr Goddard, had shown absolutely no motive whatsoever for the murder and, in effect, the only evidence that they had that Flora had committed it were the bloodstains on her clothes. After summarising the medical evidence for the jury in detail, Mr Goddard insisted that it in no way amounted to proof of guilt. He therefore suggested that the only reasonable verdict for the jury was one of acquittal.

It was left for Mr Justice Ridley to sum up the case. He reminded the jury that the only point they really needed to consider was whether or not there was any person in the house other than Flora Haskell and the victim at the time the murder was committed. Although Flora had consistently said that there was a strange man present, he had never been traced, in spite of the fact that every conceivable effort had been made to find him. Percy Noble's evidence was the key to the case, said the judge. He reiterated the point that Flora Haskell had said that Teddy had been murdered before anyone had even been upstairs to check. The murder weapon belonged to the accused and bloodstains were found on her clothes, although the judge urged the jury to treat the medical evidence with caution. No blood had been found on Flora Haskell's hands, which the judge said was a point in her favour. However, according to the prosecution, when Percy Noble knocked on the door, his aunt could well have been washing her hands in the kitchen sink.

Finally, the judge instructed the jury to exercise 'reasonable minds' on the evidence that had been presented to them. Bearing in mind that Flora Haskell had absolutely no memory of committing the murder then if the jury had any doubt about her guilt, they must acquit her.

The jury retired, returning three hours later to inform the judge that they were unable to make a decision. The judge asked if more time for deliberation would help, but the jury were adamant that they could not agree. This left Mr Justice Ridley with no alternative but to declare a mistrial and dismiss the jury. He ordered that Flora Haskell should remain in custody and face a new trial at the next Wiltshire Assizes.

The second trial opened on 2 April at Devizes, this time presided over by Mr Justice Darling. Most of the witnesses from the original trial repeated their testimony, but there was also some new evidence that had emerged in the intervening months. Miss Haskell, a sister-in-law of the defendant, had been unable to testify at the first trial. She now stated that Flora had spoken to her about her intentions to marry again and that she had also admitted 'borrowing' some of Teddy's savings to pay the rent, adding that she hoped to be able to repay it. Miss Haskell insisted that Flora had been a good mother to her son, as indeed did every single witness who testified at both trials.

Neighbour Thomas Rawlings spoke of some bloodstains that he had observed on a tablecloth downstairs. At the judge's request, Rawlings arranged a table, the cloth and three chairs as he had seen them in the defendant's home on the night of the murder. According to Rawlings, he had specifically pointed out the stains to the police superintendent in attendance, but the officer had seemed uninterested.

More medical witnesses were called and gave their opinions that Edwin's death had been caused by a single stroke of a knife across his throat, the assailant standing by the boy's head, either just above or just below him. In the former position, whoever had killed Edwin would have been in the direct line of the spray of arterial blood from the wound.

Pepper repeated his evidence that the stains on Flora Haskell's skirt and blouse could not have been the result of a knife being thrown at her in passing. William Golding again tried to justify allowing the downstairs floors to be washed in the aftermath of the murder, saying that he didn't consider that it was his duty to prevent it.

The counsels for the defence and prosecution then delivered their closing speeches, with the prosecution insisting that there had been no other person present to murder Edwin other than his mother and the defence resting on the complete absence of any motive for the murder, coupled with the numerous assertions heard in court that Flora Haskell was a good, caring, loving mother to the boy.

Mr Justice Darling then summed up the case and, if the contemporary news reports of the trial are to be believed, his summary was somewhat biased in favour of the prosecution. The judge first commended Mr Goddard on defending the prisoner with 'remarkable ability', then appeared to refute almost every aspect of the defence.

It was suggested, said Darling, that there was a man who committed the murder – but who was that man and what was his motive for killing Edwin? No money had been taken and no man who bore any ill will towards the victim had ever been found. How did Flora Haskell know that someone had killed her son before she went upstairs to check? The defence had suggested that the blood on Flora's handkerchief came from the scratch on her nose, but this was pure conjecture since Flora had never mentioned the scratch in any of her statements.

Mr Justice Darling seemed puzzled as to why Flora Haskell had not been called to the stand. Ordinarily, he said, he did not make this kind of remark, but if the prisoner could have given explanations, now was the time to make them. An opportunity had been lost by not calling the defendant to testify.

However, the jury eventually returned a verdict of 'Not Guilty on the grounds of insufficient evidence'. Flora Haskell was discharged and left the court to a background of loud cheering.

Looking at the facts of the case, as reported in the newspapers of the time, it does indeed seem strange that Flora did not give evidence in court. Why did her defence counsel, Mr Goddard, make the decision not to call her? Was he afraid of what she might reveal under cross-examination by the prosecution? Or was he not totally convinced of her innocence? Who could possibly have had a motive for killing Edwin?

Miss Haskell and Alfred Noble both testified that Flora had discussed her intentions of marrying again with them. Whoever her intended future husband was, he does not appear to have been called as a witness in court – was it possible that he wanted to marry Flora, but didn't want the additional responsibility of a disabled child? Did Edwin stand in the way of her marriage plans? Whatever the reason for his death, the murder of Edwin Richard Haskell remains unsolved.

[Note: Some contemporary sources give the date of the murder as 1 November rather than 31 October. Flora Haskell's middle name is sometimes shown as Fanny, sometimes as Annie. As the 1901 census records a Flora F. Haskell residing at her address, I have used Fanny, even though Annie is more commonly used.]

19

'I WILL MAKE THIS COUNTY RING!'

Enford, 1913

Police Constable Ernest Pike joined the force in 1895 and had since served at several police stations in Wiltshire. While serving at Bottlesford, he was promoted to sergeant and posted to Swindon police station. However, while he was undoubtedly popular within the communities that he policed, he had a quick temper, which frequently led to clashes with his superior officers.

This was the case at Swindon, where he was reported for a serious breach of discipline and brought before the Chief Constable. His wrongdoings brought about his demotion from sergeant to second class constable and an immediate transfer to the rather sleepy village of Enford, on the banks of the River Avon.

In spite of his demotion, life at Enford seemed to suit Constable Pike. He quickly settled in and got to know the community and the area very well, proving to be a very popular local 'bobby' and soon gaining back one of his stripes by being promoted to merit class constable. However, just as he had done several times in the past, he then fell foul of his superior officers, in particular Sergeant William Crouch.

Crouch was also an experienced police officer who had previously served at Bradford-upon-Avon, Swindon, Chilton Foliat and Ludgershall. A married man with two children, he now lived in the police house at Netheravon. When it came to his attention that Pike had been seen in a public house while on duty and had also lied to a superior officer, Crouch had no option but to report Pike, who once again found himself summoned to appear before the Chief Constable to explain his conduct.

The disciplinary hearing took place at Amesbury police station on 31 March 1913. Crouch presented the evidence against Pike and, although Crouch was later said to have spoken very fairly, Pike grew more and more angry as the hearing went on, eventually losing his temper and calling him a liar. When Crouch's word was believed over his and he was demoted and informed that he would have to leave Enford and take a transfer to Colerne on the county border with Somerset, Pike was enraged.

Netheravon, c. 1910. (Author's collection)

He cycled back to Enford in the company of a colleague, PC Slade, all the while fuming about the injustice of his situation, for which he placed the blame firmly on William Crouch. As the two officers reached the police house at Enford, Pike told Slade, 'Well, I have done with the Force'.

Slade advised him not to be silly, telling him 'keep yourself cool', but Pike would not be placated. As Slade remounted his bicycle to continue riding home, Pike shouted after him, 'I will make this county ring!'

Once at home, Pike appeared very dejected and sat alone brooding in the room where he kept his double-barrelled sporting gun. He left the police house to go on duty at nine o'clock that evening.

It was customary for Pike and Crouch to meet at Coombe Farm, Enford at eleven o'clock each night. On the night of 31 March, Pike apparently reached the rendezvous point first and concealed himself behind a hedge. As Crouch arrived, two shots rang out and the sergeant instantly fell to the ground, dead from gunshot wounds to his head. Mr A.L. Edwards, a doctor from Upavon, later noted that the left-hand side of Crouch's skull was almost completely blown away by the gunshot.

Meanwhile, Mrs Amelia Pike waited at the police house in Enford, growing more and more concerned about her husband by the minute. Eventually, when he didn't return home that night, she reported him missing.

While walking to work at 6 a.m. on 1 April, with a small group of farm workers, farm labourer James Cannings found the body of Sergeant William Crouch lying face down in a field known as Long Ground, close to the footpath to Fittleton. One hand was in his pocket, holding his keys, while the other was slipped into the opening of his tunic as if he had been trying to warm it. His helmet lay on the ground just in

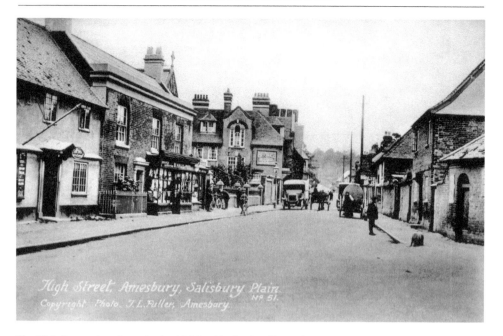

The High Street, Amesbury, in the 1920s. (Author's collection)

front of his body. Two shotgun cartridges of a similar bore and make to those used by Pike were found near the sergeant's body.

Nobody could locate Ernest Pike. PC Slade, who was stationed at Upavon, was called in to help with the search for the missing constable. Having listened to Pike's tirade of bitterness towards Crouch just the day before, Slade immediately felt that the Enford constable was responsible for the sergeant's death. He enlisted the services of two bloodhounds, Moonlight and Flair, who belonged to the Chief Constable, Captain Llewellyn. An article of Ernest Pike's clothing was obtained from his wife and the two dogs were taken to the site of Sergeant Crouch's shooting.

Although initially confused by the early morning dew, the dogs eventually led officers about 500yds through nearby water meadows to a little wooden footbridge across the River Avon, where a double-barrelled shotgun was found in the shallow water containing two cartridges, one live and one spent. The police immediately began to drag the river and soon located Pike's body, which had been carried downstream by the current for some distance before sinking to the bottom. He was dressed in his police uniform and he too had died from a gunshot wound to the head. Mr Edwards believed that Pike had placed the barrel of the shotgun in his mouth and pulled the trigger. In his opinion, both officers would have died instantly.

An inquest into the deaths of both men was opened at Coombe Farm later that day before Mr F.A.P. Sylvester, the coroner for mid-Wiltshire. The jury heard that Pike had been broken hearted on his return from his disciplinary hearing and that he seemed to blame Crouch for his demotion and transfer. It was believed that Pike had managed to remove his gun from the house without his wife noticing and that he had taken it with him when he went to meet Crouch. Whether there had been

Upavon, 1917. (Author's collection)

any argument between the two men, or whether Pike had just ambushed Crouch was not known, but the shotgun cartridges found adjacent to Crouch's body were identical to those subsequently found in Pike's desk at the police house.

Having shot Crouch, Pike would have been only too aware that he had committed a capital offence for which he would undoubtedly be hanged when apprehended. Unable to face the disgrace, he had walked to the footbridge, placed the barrel of the shotgun in his mouth and pulled the trigger. The blast had toppled him off the bridge and into the river, where his body was later found.

The inquest jury found that Ernest Pike had wilfully murdered Sergeant William Crouch and returned a verdict of *Felo de Se* against Pike (a Latin phrase meaning 'felon of himself', used in the days when it was a crime to commit suicide – the suicide victim had literally committed a crime against himself). Tragically, it emerged at the inquest that, but for the fairness of Crouch's presentation of the evidence against him at his disciplinary hearing, Pike's punishment would have been much more severe.

As a mark of respect, the inquest jury donated their fees for serving to the widows of the two police officers. The funerals of both policemen were held a few days later. Sergeant Crouch was buried with full police honours, his funeral attended by the Chief Constable and more than 150 of his fellow officers. A band from the Third Battalion of the Wiltshire Regiment played him to his grave. By contrast, Ernest Pike's funeral was a much more modest affair. Even so, it was a testament to his popularity as a community policeman that several of the villagers joined his wife and children in mourning a man who had so tragically ended two lives in what amounted to a few moments of madness.

20

'DIAGNOSIS: ALCOHOLISM'

Sutton Veny, 1917

By 1917, the First World War was gradually coming to an end. Throughout the conflict, the Army had used Salisbury Plain as a training ground for soldiers before they were sent abroad to fight on the front lines. The entire area bristled with the clusters of huts and tents used to accommodate the soldiers and all day long the surrounding countryside reverberated with the noises of war – explosions, gunfire, horses' hooves and the rumbling movement of heavy artillery.

One particular group of trainees were already far from their native land. They were young Australian soldiers, who had been sent to Sutton Veny to learn how to use Lewis machine guns at the firing range there.

Two of the instructors charged with teaching the young recruits were also Australian. Verney Asser, aged thirty, and Corporal Joseph Harold Durkin, aged twenty-four, shared a hut and, at one stage, were both competing for the affections of the same woman. Durkin won that particular competition and, in spite of the fact that he had a fiancée back home in Australia, began to see the young English widow on a regular basis. Asser seemed to accept the situation and the two men were, to all intents and purposes, on friendly terms.

In November 1917, Durkin wrote to his English girlfriend asking her to visit him at camp on the evening of 28 November. On the day before her expected visit, he and Asser went to the canteen together. Both seemed to be in good spirits as they ate their food before retiring to their hut for the night.

At some time during the evening, Durkin probably told Asser that the young woman was coming the next day and at 9.30 p.m., Asser left the hut and went to the nearby ammunition store, where he asked the officer in charge, Corporal Milne, if he might have some empty magazines. He was told to help himself.

Just minutes later, as Milne was getting ready for bed, he was startled by the sound of a shot from the direction of Asser and Durkin's hut. Immediately after the noise, a bullet came through the wall of Milne's hut, passed through a haversack and a tunic, and then went out through the opposite wall of the hut.

Two views of Sutton Veny, c. 1910. (Author's collection)

Assuming the shot had been fired accidentally, Milne did nothing about it and went to bed. Asser was to make a further two visits to the ammunition store before 11 p.m., rummaging around in the area where the Lewis gun ammunition was kept for a few moments then leaving abruptly. Milne was unaware if he had taken anything. Ten minutes later, there was a second shot from Asser's hut and, shortly afterwards, at just after 11 p.m., Asser went to the guardhouse to report that Durkin had shot himself.

Durkin was found lying on his right-hand side in his bed in the hut. He was undressed and the bedclothes were pulled up as if he had been sleeping normally. His arms were outstretched and his rifle lay across his wrists. A bullet had entered his left cheek, exiting just below his right ear. The spent cartridge had been ejected from the rifle after it had been fired.

Asser told officers that he had been awakened from sleep by the sound of the shot and, having struck a match, had realised immediately that Durkin had shot himself. Almost as a reflex action, he had taken the rifle from him and ejected the cartridge before replacing the weapon where he had found it. However, aspects of Asser's explanation just didn't ring true.

It was noticed that his bed had not been made up and that the bedding was still in its roll, making it unlikely that he had been sleeping. When this was pointed out to Asser, he explained that he had been asleep on the floor. In addition, when Asser had alerted the sergeant about Durkin's alleged suicide, he was fully dressed in his uniform, including his boots and puttees. The guards felt it highly unlikely that, had he been asleep at the time the shot was fired, he would have lingered for long enough to completely dress himself before calling for assistance.

The shooting was reported to the civilian police and an inquest into the death of Corporal Durkin was opened on the following day. At the inquest, Asser stated that Durkin had been depressed about his engagement to his Australian fiancée and his relationship with the young English widow. The jury returned a verdict of suicide.

Meanwhile, Superintendent Scott of the local police force had visited the scene of the shooting and he too had doubts that Durkin had committed suicide, believing instead that he had been murdered. When the wound on Durkin's face was examined, it showed no traces of gunpowder residue or burning at the point of entry of the bullet, indicating that the muzzle had not been in direct contact with Durkin's skin when the rifle was fired. Even if the weapon had been pressed tight against his cheek, the trigger would then have been impossible for Durkin to reach since he had particularly short arms.

Scott decided to conduct some experiments and obtained some cuts of mutton, which were used to represent human flesh. The rifle was loaded with identical ammunition to that which had killed Durkin and test fired at the joints of meat from varying distances. It was found that, when the rifle was fired with its muzzle about 5in away, a wound similar in appearance to that of Durkin's wound was produced on the meat.

With the gun muzzle 5in away from his face, Durkin could not possibly have pulled the trigger with his finger. The only way he could have committed suicide was by using a toe to fire the gun and he was found tucked into bed, covered by his bedclothes.

As a result of the ballistics experiments, Asser was arrested on 3 December 1917 for the murder of Corporal Joseph Harold Durkin. He was tried at Devizes on 15 January 1918 before Mr Justice Avory, with J.A. Foote and T.H. Parr prosecuting and S.H. Emmanuel defending.

Asser continued to claim in court that he had retired to bed at about 9.40 p.m. on the night of Durkin's death and had slept soundly until he was disturbed by the fatal shot. He denied visiting the ammunition store and also denied firing the wayward shot that had travelled through the ammunition store as Corporal Milne had prepared for bed. Asked why he had ejected the cartridge from the rifle, Asser replied that he didn't know, arguing that removing the cartridge was probably a normal reaction that would have been done by any soldier. Yet this argument didn't explain why he had then replaced the rifle as he purported to have found it, lying across Durkin's wrists. Asser was also unable to give a satisfactory explanation for the fact that his bed had not been slept in, nor was he able to explain why he had stopped to dress himself before seeking assistance for his comrade.

The counsel for the prosecution reminded the jury of the results of the experiments carried out using the murder weapon and the joints of mutton, which had clearly indicated that it would have been a physical impossibility for Durkin to shoot himself, given his short arms and the fact that his feet and legs were covered by his bedclothes. The only problem that the prosecution encountered was in trying to establish a motive for the murder. Durkin and Asser had quarrelled in the past and were also rivals for the affections of the same woman, yet there was no indication that Asser had been jealous.

In his summing up for the jury, Mr Justice Avory told them that the case boiled down to whether the jury accepted Asser's account of events or Corporal Milne's.

The High Street, Sutton Veny, 1917. (Author's collection)

At the end of the two-day trial, it took the jury just ninety minutes to decide that they favoured Milne's version and find Verney Asser guilty.

Asser was sentenced to death for the wilful murder of Corporal Durkin, but Mr Emmanuel immediately appealed against the conviction on the grounds that no insanity defence had been considered at the trial.

Emmanuel claimed that the only material he was given at the trial relating to the defendant's mental state was a military record sheet on which it was noted that, in July 1916, Asser had been admitted to hospital for 'mental derangement' and remained an in-patient for four days. There had been no opportunity at the trial for the defence team to investigate further, but enquiries had been made since the end of the court case that had both confirmed the admission and offered an explanation for the symptoms of mental derangement, with the stark words 'Diagnosis: alcoholism'.

The counsel for the defence had found evidence of insanity in Asser's immediate family, his father having committed suicide some years previously. The defendant himself had been an inmate of various asylums and mental hospitals. He also claimed to have previously enlisted as a bugler boy on one of his Majesty's ships but to have been discharged due to suffering from dementia. Records did show that a boy called James Nugent had been discharged from the services under these circumstances and Asser claimed that he was the James Nugent concerned and that he had enlisted in the Army under a different name to avoid the military authorities finding out that he had been treated in a lunatic asylum.

Asser maintained that, if he had actually committed the act for which he had been sentenced then he could not have been responsible for his actions. However, the Court of Criminal Appeal was of the opinion that they were being asked to consider evidence that had not been brought up in the original trial and this was not within their power. Only the Home Office could legitimately rule on the sanity or insanity of the defendant and therefore the appeal was dismissed.

The fact that the Home Secretary made no intervention against Asser's sentence is evidenced by his execution, carried out by John Ellis on 5 March 1918 at Shepton Mallet prison.

[Note: In contemporary accounts of the murder, Verney Asser is also referred to as Verney Hasser. The two variations of the name appear almost equally – I have used the spelling Asser as it appears in both *The Times* and in the online History of the Wiltshire Constabulary.]

21

'I DONE THE JOB AND AM PREPARED TO STAND THE CONSEQUENCES'

Long Newnton, 1924

The village of Long Newnton lies almost on the border between Gloucestershire and Wiltshire. The moving of the county boundary in 1930 left the village in Gloucestershire, although in 1925 it was still a part of Wiltshire and it was in a field there, on the Malmesbury Road, that thirty-seven-year-old Margaret Legg met an untimely end.

Margaret Legg was a married woman with one child, and lived in Florence Street, Swindon. In 1917, she had been out with a friend when she had met William Grover Bignell, who was then serving in the Army. There had been an immediate attraction between the two and, having told William that she was unmarried, Margaret promptly moved into his lodgings with him. Within two weeks she had left him and gone back to her husband, leaving Bignell with a venereal disease to remember her by.

In spite of this, William and Margaret kept in touch with each other both by letter and by frequent visits that Bignell made to her house and, in October 1924, Margaret asked William to move into her marital home, promising to find some way of explaining his presence to her husband. Thus, on 23 October 1924, William Bignell moved in with Margaret Legg and her family.

By the next day, Margaret was declaring her undying love for William and telling her neighbours that they were planning to run away together. In William's hearing, she told one neighbour, Mrs Drury, that if she didn't go away with him then he would commit suicide. Mrs Drury told Margaret Legg that she was a fool, but nevertheless, Margaret and William left Swindon together on 25 October.

Market Square, Tetbury, in the 1920s. (Author's collection)

By nine o'clock, the couple had reached Tetbury in Gloucestershire, where they called in at the Fox Inn. William ordered a pint of beer for himself and a glass of stout for Margaret. The two sat in the pub for almost an hour enjoying their drinks and seeming to the other customers to be on the best of terms. They left the pub together at 9.55 p.m. and by 10.30 p.m. William Bignell was in the market square in Tetbury alone, asking Police Sergeant Merritt where he might get a 'doss'. Commenting that Bignell had left it a bit late to look for lodgings, the sergeant suggested that he tried the fish shop and the pub, both of which were known to let rooms. Bignell wandered off, returning to speak to Merritt again some minutes later. He told Merritt that he had had no luck, and suggested that Merritt should lock him up, to which Merritt replied that he had nothing to lock him up for. He asked where Bignell came from and was told Wotton-under-Edge. 'You are a young man,' the sergeant told Bignell. 'Brace yourself up and walk home.'

'No fear! I am not walking to Wotton-under-Edge for you or anyone else. You have got to lock me up.'

Bignell went off again, but didn't go far. Merritt saw him talking to a small group of people and, having heard Bignell ask them where the police station was, Merritt went over and was again asked by Bignell if he would lock him up. Merritt repeated that he had no reason to do so then could hardly believe his ears when Bignell calmly said, 'I have killed a woman.'

Merritt put his hand on Bignell's shoulder and advised him to be careful what he was saying, but Bignell insisted that he was telling the truth. Realising now that Bignell's hands and clothes were bloodstained, Merritt looked at the group of people that Bignell had been talking to and singled out Wilfred Peer. 'I want you to come with me as I think something has happened,' he told him and the three men set off to walk back along the Malmsebury road.

When they reached Long Newnton, Bignell stopped at a field gate. 'This is the place,' he assured the sergeant and directed the men to a hedge, beneath which lay the body of a woman. Her throat was cut and a handkerchief had been tied so tightly around her neck that part of it was deeply embedded in the wound. A bloody, half-opened razor lay on the grass, a few feet from the body.

Bignell suddenly became upset, shouting, 'Meg, Meg,' then saying, 'oh, she's dead'. He turned to Sergeant Merritt and asked him if he believed him now. Merritt could see with his own eyes that he had no reason to doubt Bignell's assertions. He arrested Bignell and, leaving Peer guarding the body, escorted Bignell to the police station at Tetbury. Soon Superintendent Zebedee arrived with a car to convey the prisoner to the police station at Malmesbury for further questioning and, when they arrived, cautioned Bignell to be careful not to fall getting out of the car. 'I shall have a longer drop than this and the sooner the better,' Bignell told him. 'I done the job and am prepared to stand the consequences.'

A post-mortem examination on Margaret Legg conducted by Dr Richard Sedgwick of Tetbury showed that she had died as a result of blood loss, the right-hand side of her throat having been deeply cut. There were no signs of a struggle in the field at Long Newnton and Sedgwick theorised that Margaret had been surprised, attacked from behind by her killer who had drawn the razor once across her throat, using considerable force.

Given Bignell's confession to the murder and the fact that he had willingly led the police to the body, his appearance before magistrates was a mere formality and he was committed to stand trial at the next Wiltshire Assizes. The trial opened on 20 January 1925, under Mr Justice Roche. G.D. Roberts and E.A. Hawke prosecuted while Reginald Holt had the thankless task of defending the obviously guilty Bignell.

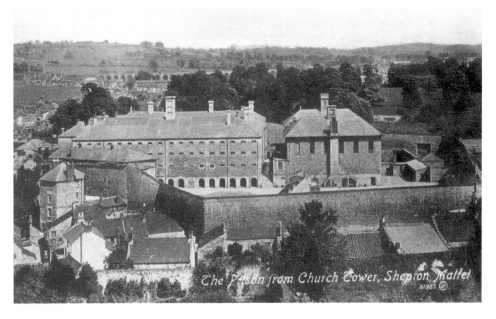

Shepton Mallet prison, 1918. (Author's collection)

As a matter of course, Bignell pleaded 'Not Guilty' to the wilful murder of Margaret Legg. The prosecution called Margaret's neighbour, Mrs Drury, and Wilfred Peer, as well as the police officers who had been involved with Bignell's arrest. A bundle of letters was produced in court, one of which was read out as an illustration of the content of them all. They were affectionate letters written by Margaret Legg to William Bignell.

It was then left to the defence to find some mitigating circumstances for Bignell's actions and Mr Holt chose to focus on his client's mental state at the time of the murder. He pointed out to the court that Bignell's mind was impaired due to a 'certain disease' – the venereal disease that he had caught from the dead woman in 1908. However, two medical witnesses disagreed with Holt's statements. One argued that, while such a disease might conceivably cause a general paralysis of the brain, he would have not expected such symptoms to appear for many years after the person was first infected. The medical officer at Shepton Mallet prison, who had observed Bignell since he was first incarcerated, told the court that, as far as he could see, Bignell was quite normal mentally.

Undeterred, Holt produced a further two witnesses to strengthen his argument that Bignell was insane at the time of the murder. The first, appropriately called Mrs Brain, who lived in Wotton-under-Edge, was a cousin of the defendant. She testified to a family history of insanity, telling the court that Bignell's mother, now dead, had attempted suicide and his brother had died an imbecile in a mental asylum. Bignell, said Mrs Brain, had always been somewhat strange in his manner, particularly so on the last occasion on which she saw him, which was on the Saturday before the murder.

Holt also called PC Crook, the village constable at Wotton-under-Edge, who had interviewed Bignell in March 1913 after it had been reported that he had returned to his lodgings wet through. At that time, Bignell had told Crook that he had tried to drown himself because he was out of work and destitute. Crook had found him a place in a Poor Law establishment where Bignell had lived on and off ever since.

Having heard all the evidence, Mr Justice Roche summed up the case for the jury, paying particular attention to the laws appertaining to the plea of insanity. The jury retired for twenty minutes before returning to say that they had found the prisoner guilty of wilful murder with no evidence of insanity.

Asked by the judge if he had anything to say why sentence should not be passed, Bignell cheerfully replied, 'No, I think it is a very good verdict'. He was then sentenced to execution.

Thomas Pierrepoint carried out the sentence at Shepton Mallet prison on 24 February 1925, assisted by Robert Baxter. Thirty-two-year-old Bignell went to the scaffold still seemingly unconcerned by his fate, leaving behind him the unanswered questions of why he killed thirty-seven-year-old Margaret Legg and whether his willing confession to the murder was made only because he desperately needed a place to sleep and saw a police cell as a more comfortable alternative to a long walk home on a cold October night.

22

'YOU HAVE GOT ME, YOU ROTTER'

Trowbridge, 1925

On the day before Christmas Eve 1925, commercial traveller Edward Charles Ingram Richards met his colleague Samuel Gay at 7.30 p.m. The two men worked for Usher's Brewery and spent the evening calling on hotels in the Bath area, collecting orders and payments. Having enjoyed their supper at one of the hotels, the two men worked until closing time when they went on to a club, where they stayed chatting to friends until just after 11 p.m. By then, the weather had deteriorated somewhat and it was past midnight when they reached the garage at Trowbridge where Richards normally kept his company car.

After writing out some orders for the brewery, Richards and Gay parted company, each setting off in opposite directions to walk home. Richards had about a mile to walk to his house in Victoria Road and as the brewery office was now closed, he took the night's takings with him for safekeeping.

Richards shared his home with another brewery employer, Walter Stourton, who, with his wife, sublet the front part of the house. That evening, the Stourtons had retired to bed at about 10.30 p.m. and appeared to be sleeping soundly. Then Walter was disturbed by the sound of something being thrown at his bedroom window. When he woke up, he could hear a voice shouting, 'Wal, come on down.'

Recognising the voice as that of his landlord, Walter didn't bother to get up immediately. Thinking that Richards had simply forgotten his key, he called out to tell him that the back door was unlocked, but Richards was insistent that Walter should come downstairs so he reluctantly got out of bed, lit a candle and put on a few clothes.

As he walked downstairs, he heard a loud noise as if someone were hammering on the back door. The downstairs of the house was in darkness and, as Walter paused to light the gas lamps in the scullery, he noticed that the back door was open. As the light from the lamps spilled outside, Walter spotted Richards lying on his back in the garden.

As Walter approached him, Richards weakly told him, 'They've got me, Wal.'

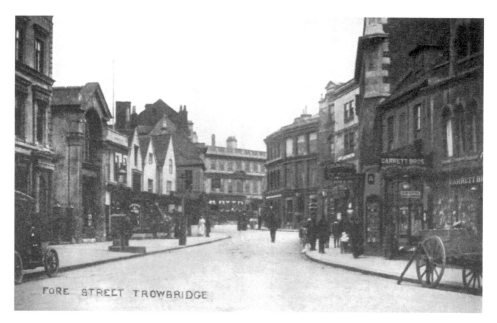

Fore Street, Trowbridge, in the 1920s. (Author's collection)

Victoria Road, Trowbridge, 2008. (© N. Sly)

'What do you mean, they've got you?' asked Stourton, probably still suspecting that his landlord had imbibed a little too much alcohol.

'They've shot me. It was two men,' replied Richards.

As Stourton turned to go back to the house for a more powerful light, he was aware of a motorcycle starting up a little way along the road, its headlight briefly illuminating the night as it pulled away in the direction of Hilperton Road.

Stourton grabbed his bicycle lamp and knelt at Richards's side. He could see that Richards was bleeding from a wound in his head and that he was tightly clutching a revolver in his right hand. As Stourton took the weapon, he could smell that it had recently been fired. He tried to lift Richards, but he was too heavy, so he rushed back indoors for a cushion to put under his landlord's head. Having made Richards as comfortable as he could, Walter summoned assistance.

When the police arrived on the scene, Superintendent Alf Underwood asked Richards what the problem was, to which Richards replied, 'They kicked me in the stomach.' By now, the injured man seemed to be in a great deal of pain, writhing on the ground, groaning and clutching his stomach. Nevertheless, as they waited for medical help to arrive, he was able to tell the police that there had been two men waiting in the house for him when he got home, one tall, one short. Underwood noticed Richards's wallet protruding from one of his hip pockets, still containing £40 10s in bank notes and five cheques totalling £178 3s 4d.

Dr Michael Wright gave Richards what first aid he could in the cold, dark garden, and then travelled with him to hospital. During the journey, Richards was able to give more information about the attack, telling the doctor that he had fired his own gun once, not at the intruders but just to frighten them. He did not know the identity of the two men.

Richards died from his injuries within minutes of being admitted to hospital. A post-mortem examination, carried out by Dr Walter Hall, the Professor of Pathology at Bristol University, revealed three wounds on the left-hand side of Richards's head, all three penetrating to the bone. In addition, Richards had a single bullet wound to the left of his breastbone, the bullet having passed through one of his lungs and his heart.

When Richards was lifted from the garden to be taken to hospital, a cartridge case and a bullet were found on the ground close to where he had first been discovered by Stourton. A search of the house revealed a .32 cartridge case in the kitchen, two more just inside the back door and a further three outside, between the back door and a greenhouse. There were shot marks on the back door jamb, a bullet hole above the door that led from the scullery to the kitchen, and two more bullet holes in the post of a garden archway. Richards's revolver contained one empty cartridge case and one live cartridge, which were different to the ones found in the house and garden.

The police began their investigations at the nearby barracks of the Royal Horse Artillery, where they checked leave records for the night of the murder. Two bombardiers were found to have been absent from the barracks during the relevant time and, when it was discovered that one of them knew Richards and was aware of his normal routines, both were taken in for questioning. Ian Ronald Maxwell Stewart, aged twenty, and twenty-three-year-old Ignatius Emanuel Napthali Trebitsch Lincoln – otherwise known as John Lincoln – were subsequently charged when a spot of fresh blood was found on Lincoln's raincoat. After appearing before magistrates at Trowbridge, both were committed for trial at the Assizes in Devizes.

The trial opened on 20 January 1926, before Mr Justice Talbot. It quickly became evident that there was insufficient evidence to convict Stewart and, in addition, nothing to suggest that he had been aware that Lincoln was armed prior to entering Richards's house. At the direction of the judge, he was acquitted but immediately indicted for robbery with violence.

Lincoln was one of the first to give evidence. He told the court that his father was Hungarian and his mother German and that his eldest brother, Julius, was head of the Criminal Investigation Department of the British Army in Germany.

John Lincoln had travelled widely overseas and had got into the habit of carrying a revolver for his own protection. On 23 December of the previous year, Stewart had suggested that the two men went to Richards's house with the intention of robbing him. Having drunk a considerable quantity of rum, the two men went to Victoria Road finding the house in darkness and Richards obviously not at home. Realising that the back door was unlocked, they decided to search the house to see if they could find any items of value, with Stewart eventually finding a small revolver in the living room, which he put in his pocket.

A cupboard under the stairs yielded a half-bottle of brandy, which the two men shared, along with a crate of bottled beer. They were each enjoying their first bottle of beer when they heard the back door opening and, before they could react, a voice said 'The game's up' and a shot was fired.

Telling the court that, by this time, not only was he feeling the effects of the large quantity of alcohol that he had consumed but was also in a 'frenzy' at having been shot at, Lincoln described how he had run to the front door of the house, but had been unable to escape because it was locked. He then ran to the back door, poked the muzzle of his gun through the gap between the edge of the door and the wall and fired three shots in rapid succession. He maintained that he had not aimed the gun at anyone since he had not been able to see where he was firing – instead he had fired towards the ground with the sole intention of frightening the person who had opened the door, so that he and Stewart could make good their escape. Stewart had then bolted out of the back door, disappearing from sight round the corner of the house. Lincoln had followed him more cautiously, keeping close to the house wall. As he had reached the end of the wall, another shot had been fired at him, so he had raised his gun and fired in the general direction from which it came.

A voice from the darkness said, 'you have got me, you rotter', so Lincoln had gone towards the voice, his revolver now empty. A man had suddenly run at him out of the darkness and, finding himself still clutching the beer bottle, Lincoln had instinctively swung it at the man's head, at which the man had staggered and dropped to the floor. He was adamant that he had been unaware that he had actually shot Richards, but believed that he had merely knocked him unconscious.

Mr Hemmerde KC for the defence told the jury that Lincoln was guilty of manslaughter rather than murder, since he was so befuddled with drink and terror at the time of the shooting and had not deliberately aimed his gun at Richards but had fired and hit him accidentally. He described Lincoln's reasoning as 'so dethroned' and abnormal that it was inconceivable that he would have been able to form the intent that was the very essence of murder.

Hemmerde then went on to address Lincoln's family background. His father was Ignatius Timothy Trebitsch-Lincoln, an eccentric, who served as the Liberal MP for Darlington for eleven months during 1910. Finding the life of an MP too poorly paid, he did not stand for re-election at the general election of November 1910.

After his brief career in politics, Trebitsch-Lincoln tried his hand at a number of commercial enterprises with little success. At the outbreak of the First World War, he offered his services to the British government as a spy and, when he was turned down, he travelled to Holland and made contact with the Germans, for whom he worked as a double agent. He was eventually tracked down and returned to England, charged with fraud. He served three years in Parkhurst Prison on the Isle of Wight before being deported in 1919. Hemmerde said that he hoped the jury would not let the accused man's 'unfortunate parentage' affect their decision in any way.

The judge then summed up the case for the jury, telling them that it was impossible to consider the shooting of Edward Richards as anything other than wilful murder and pointing out that wilful murder did not mean that the perpetrator had schemed beforehand to kill. Addressing Lincoln's mental state at the time of the shooting, he conceded that this was a matter for the jury to consider during their deliberations, adding that he was bound to say that he saw no foundations for any defence of that kind in this case. As to the effects of liquor: drunkenness was no defence whatsoever if it simply meant that the defendant was so drunk that he did something that he would not ordinarily have done if sober.

It took the jury just fifteen minutes to arrive at a verdict of 'Guilty'. Asked if he had anything to say before he was sentenced, Lincoln replied simply, 'No'. Mr Justice Talbot told him that he had, by his actions, cut off the life of a young, happy, prosperous man for which he would forfeit his own young life which, but for his wicked folly, might have also been happy and useful.

With Lincoln sentenced to death, his place in the dock was taken by Stewart, who, in front of a new jury, was indicted for robbery with violence. Once again, the charge against him was dismissed and Stewart was discharged, only to be immediately rearrested for burglary.

Stewart was brought before magistrates at Trowbridge on 4 February 1926. His defence counsel, Mr Wansbrough, immediately objected on the grounds that Stewart had not been cautioned after his arrest in the court, hence Wansbrough argued that any statements made by the accused after his arrest should be disallowed. Regardless, Stewart was committed for trial at Winchester Assizes, where Mr Justice Roche subsequently sentenced him to fourteen years penal servitude. The sentence was later appealed but upheld.

Lincoln's sentence was also appealed on the grounds that due consideration had not been given to his drunkenness and his abnormal state of mind at the time of the shooting. Lincoln's brother Julius came to England from Germany in support of the appeal and a petition was raised asking the local MP, Captain Walter Shaw, to bring what was described as 'a grave error of justice' to the attention of Parliament. However, the appeal court found that the judge had clearly advised the jury to consider Lincoln's mental state during their deliberations and could find nothing to justify a reduction of the charge from murder to manslaughter and no reason to commute Lincoln's death sentence to one of life imprisonment. Accordingly, Thomas Pierrepoint executed Ignatius Emanuel Napthali Trebitsch Lincoln at Shepton Mallet prison on 2 March 1926.

[Note: The brewery clerk with whom Richards travelled on the evening before his death is referred to in cotemporary accounts of the murder as both Samuel Gay and Samuel Gray.]

23

'I'LL SEE SHE SHAN'T LIVE TO HAVE THE LAUGH OVER ME'

Durrington, 1939

William Hugh Cousins, aged forty-four, was a married man with four children, but for ten years he had been living apart from his wife and family. His wife, Mary Ann Cousins, lived with the children at a cottage in Durrington, while William lived as man and wife with Miss Edith Jessie Cable at Laburnum Cottages in Alderbury. Miss Cable had three children, the youngest of whom was born in 1921 and was fathered by William Cousins.

Cousins desperately wanted his wife to grant him a divorce so that he could marry Miss Cable, but Mary Ann was a staunch Roman Catholic and divorce was against her religious beliefs. Besides which, even though he had left her ten years ago, Mary Ann still seemed to hold out hopes of a reconciliation with her husband.

Mr and Mrs Cousins spoke on the telephone on 5 June 1939 and whatever the conversation between them, it prompted William to write a registered letter to his wife. The letter was headed 'Please do not stand in my way of happiness and justice' and continued:

Dear Mother,
With reference to our conversation this morning re to come and live together again, I cannot see no matter how I have tried of my ever living happy with you and after what I have done does not wish to come back again to you even when your ten lodgers has gone. But you could make me happy if you tried and forgave me for my wrong doings. But please take this as final. I cannot ever go back again. There is only left for me one way out if you don't take divorce proceedings against me. I must do something, even if it costs me all I have got and that is not much. From your broken-hearted husband. Please don't ask me to come back at any future date. I cannot.
Yours W.H. Cousins. [*sic*]

In May of that year, Edith Cable had become ill and on 22 May she was admitted to Salisbury hospital where she underwent an operation on her stomach. She was discharged to a convalescent home in Bournemouth, where she was due to stay until 13 July. At first Edith Cable and William Cousins continued to exchange affectionate letters but on 8 July, Edith suddenly seemed to change. She wrote to Cousins advising him that she wanted to end their relationship and to be alone, asking him to arrange for her clothes to be packed up so that she could collect them when she left the convalescent home.

Cousins had driven to Bournemouth to see Edith Cable on 8 July and the two had gone out together in the car. On 9 July, Cousins again appeared at the Convalescent Home and Miss Cable was seen to go out to his car to meet him. It was the last time that she was to be seen alive.

At about half past nine on the evening of 9 July, William's daughter, Kathleen Cousins, arrived home and found her father in conversation with her mother in the kitchen. Kathleen went upstairs and shortly afterwards Mary Ann joined her in her bedroom, speaking briefly to Kathleen before returning downstairs. Whatever Mary Ann said to Kathleen obviously worried the girl since she immediately decided to go downstairs herself. She had just got to the top of the stairs when she heard a gunshot, followed by a shout from her mother of 'Kath. Kath. He has shot me!' then a second shot. William Cousins immediately called out to Kathleen telling her not to come into the kitchen, but to send one of the lodgers in instead.

As a way of earning more money, having to bring up her children alone, Mary Ann Cousins had let some rooms to boarders. Now, in addition to her family, there were four male lodgers in the house, all of whom had been asleep in their bedrooms at the time of the shooting.

John O'Brien – one of three cousins all named O'Brien who were lodging with Mrs Cousins and her children – was awakened by a woman screaming at just after half past nine. Moments later, Kathleen Cousins burst into his bedroom, in a state of panic. The three O'Brien's ran to alert Samuel Fiddler, the fourth lodger. As Fiddler got up, he heard a man's voice shout cheerfully from downstairs, 'Come on down, you Irish boys.'

Fiddler followed the O'Brien's down to the kitchen. As John and Timothy O'Brien opened the kitchen door, they were greeted by William Cousins, who calmly told them, 'Take this gun, go to the police station and fetch a policeman. I have shot my wife.'

John O'Brien took the gun and passed it to Samuel Fiddler, who was still coming downstairs at the time. Fiddler went back up to his room and left the gun safely there then made his way to the kitchen. As he entered the kitchen, William Cousins approached him and shook his hand telling him, 'This is the third I have done.' He then asked Fiddler if he would stay on and look after the children. Fiddler saw Mrs Cousins' body lying on the floor, covered by a tablecloth, and set off for the police station at Durrington. He arrived there soon after the O'Brien's and, within minutes, Constable Zebedee was driving to the house, with PC Pierce following in another car.

As soon as Zebedee arrived, he saw Mrs Cousins' body and removed the tablecloth to see if he could render any first aid, but the woman was clearly dead. Hearing a voice from upstairs, Zebedee shouted to ask if it was Mr Cousins. 'Yes. I am just coming down,' replied Cousins.

Durrington in the 1920s. (Author's collection)

Cousins came into the kitchen and shook hands with PC Zebedee. 'I am going to make things as easy for you as I can,' he told the constable. There is only one way out of this. I have lived a man and I will die a man. My wife lies dead on the mat there. I shot her just now.' Zebedee tried to caution him, but Cousins was determined to have his say. 'I know I shall hang for this,' he continued, 'but I don't mind that. Out in the yard in a car is another dead woman, the woman I love. I strangled her at Ringwood at ten to eight tonight. After I had strangled her and driven about 100 yards, I thought I saw her move, so I shot her.' Just then Mrs Cousins appeared to make a slight movement, an involuntary twitch of the muscles. Immediately William snatched a whisky bottle from the table and threw it at his wife's head. 'She is not dead yet,' he explained to the startled policeman. 'Give me the gun again. I'll see she shan't live to have the laugh over me.'

Cousins then handed a .410 gun cartridge to PC Zebedee telling him that, although he had given the gun to the lodgers, since they were all Irish like his wife, he had been too frightened to give them the cartridge in case they shot him.

When PC Pierce arrived at the cottage, Cousins greeted him cordially, almost as if he were an invited guest. He knew Pierce and insisted on shaking his hand, telling him, 'I have just killed my wife. Or at least, I hope I have.' Pierce cautioned Cousins not to say any more, but Cousins insisted, saying, 'I want to help you all I can.'

He then led the officers to his car parked in the yard outside and unlocked the front passenger side door. Edith Cable was sitting in the passenger seat, her body covered by a coat, on the lap of which had been scattered a bunch of sweet peas. Cousins pulled back the coat and gently kissed Edith Cable before locking the car door again and passing the key to the police.

Cousins was taken to Amesbury police station and a thorough search was made of his car. A spent cartridge was found in the back, along with three empty quart bottles of beer and a glass that had obviously been used. The police also found numerous letters in the car, some of which were correspondence between Cousins and Edith Cable and one that was addressed to the chief of police, Salisbury. The letter was dated Wednesday 21 June 1939 and related that Cousins wanted to finish this 'horrific life' as he had been deprived of the woman he wished to marry. He had always said that only death would part himself and Miss Cable and it was true. Cousins wrote that he had no intention of committing suicide, but intended to die on Winchester Scaffold with a good heart for the woman he loved.

Charged on the following morning with the murders of Edith Cable and Mary Ann Cousins, William Cousins professed himself to be 'exceptionally glad' and 'as happy as a sand lark' and only wished he could have 'got the other three', although he did not specify who those three might be.

An inquest into the deaths of the two women was opened at the Amesbury Public Assistance Union before County Coroner Mr H. Dale. It was a particularly poignant occasion as William Cousins junior, William and Mary Ann's son, had been married only that morning. Obviously, neither his father nor his mother had attended his wedding, which should have been a happy family occasion.

The bodies of the two dead women had been taken by ambulance to the mortuary at Amesbury and, according to Dr Neighbour, both had still been warm on arrival. He had conducted a post-mortem examination on both women, finding them to have suffered gunshot wounds that could not have been self-inflicted. Edith Cable had also been partially asphyxiated before being shot. The deaths of both women were attributed to gunshot wounds and resultant shock.

After hearing evidence of formal identification and the medical evidence, the coroner adjourned the inquest pending the outcome of criminal proceedings. Meanwhile, Cousins made three appearances before magistrates at Salisbury before being committed for trial at the next Wiltshire Assizes.

His trial opened before Mr Justice Croom-Johnson at Devizes, with Mr Scott Henderson prosecuting and Mr J. Skelhorn and Mr M. Hughes appearing for the defence. Cousins, who was tried only for the murder of his wife, pleaded 'Not Guilty'.

As expected, much of the trial focused on Cousins' mental state at the time of the murder, with the defence offering a plea of insanity. It was the prosecution's contention that a man was assumed to be sane unless he is proved otherwise and the counsel for the prosecution pointedly asked several witnesses about Cousins' conduct at the time of the murder. His daughter, Kathleen, described him as 'exceptionally calm' and 'barely agitated'. PC Zebedee testified that, as far as he was concerned, Cousins' conduct did not seem strange, although he conceded that the defendant throwing a whisky bottle at his dead wife's head had seemed somewhat unusual at the time.

The defence called several witnesses to testify on the subject of Cousins' mental state. The first of these was Mr A.B. Lemon, a solicitor who had acted professionally for Cousins for about ten years. Lemon had seen his client a few days before the murders and stated that, at that time, he had been very strange in his manner. Normally a quiet, gentle man, Lemon believed that Cousins was distraught and

Wiltshire | GEORGE JARDINE KIDSTON, Esquire, C.M.G.,
TO WIT. | Sheriff of the County aforesaid,

To Robert William Morgan,

of 1, Middlelands, Downton.

You are hereby required to be and appear at the Assizes to be holden at Salisbury, in and for the County aforesaid, on *Wednesday*, the *Fourteenth* day of *October* 1936, at *Eleven* o'clock in the forenoon precisely, *and so on from day to day until discharged by order of the Court*, to serve as one of the JURORS, to be impanelled and duly sworn at the said Assizes, for the Trial of all issues Criminal, which may then and there come on for Trial. Hereof fail not.

Given under the Seal of his Office, the *Twenty-Ninth* day of *September*, One Thousand Nine Hundred and Thirty-six.

Neville J. Awdry,

Under Sheriff,

Chippenham.

Wiltshire Assizes jury form, dating from 1936. (Author's collection)

more than capable of becoming violent. He had been so concerned by his client's uncharacteristic behaviour that he had requested that a clerk remain in the office while he was dealing with Cousins. He had hurried through his business with the defendant then ushered Cousins out of the office as soon as he politely could. On that occasion, the purpose of the meeting between the solicitor and his client had been to discuss a possible divorce and Lemon had advised Cousins that the chances of him getting a divorce from his wife were pretty slim.

The defence next called Dr Arthur Guirdham, the head of a private mental hospital and a specialist in diseases of the mind. He had examined Cousins on 29 September and stated that Cousins had continued to insist that he was 'very happy'. In conversation, Cousins tended to wander wildly off topic, harping on about trivial details of the First World War rather than sticking to the point. The doctor told the court that Cousins had suffered from severe headaches after a motorcycle accident five years earlier and also complained of cold, numb feelings starting around his heart and spreading around his body. He had been oversensitive and unreasonably afraid of a standard eye test using a torch. Although he had eventually been convinced that it was a harmless routine procedure, he had continued to show irrational fear, trembling and becoming agitated when the test was repeated. Guirdham's diagnosis was that Cousins was mentally abnormal and suffered from schizophrenia. The main manifestations were that he did not react to particular sets of emotional cues in the way a normal person would do. The doctor gave the example that something that may make a normal person depressed might possibly have the opposite effect on Cousins.

The disease would affect Cousins' ability to differentiate between right and wrong and, in the case of the murder of his wife, Cousins was even now totally convinced that he had done right rather than wrong. The doctor told the court that Cousins believed that his wife had been unfaithful to him and that two of her four children had been fathered by another man. 'That might not be a delusion at all,' interjected the judge, who wanted clarification as to whether or not Cousins knew right from wrong when he shot his wife. The doctor drew the court's attention to the letter that Cousins had written to the chief of police, in which he had stated that he was prepared to die on the gallows. Cousins clearly knew that what he was doing was against the law of the land, but his disease had affected his values, making the act seem not wrong in his mind.

Dr Guirdham was prepared to say that he believed that Cousins was completely insane at the time that he killed both his wife and Edith Cable. His opinion was backed up by Dr R.F. Barbour of Bristol, who had examined Cousins on four occasions and had consequently diagnosed paranoid schizophrenia.

The prosecution had also called a medical witness, Dr Hugh Grierson, the senior medical officer at Wandsworth Prison. He had agreed that Cousins was suffering from a mental illness, but believed that it was in its very early stage. Describing Cousins as of 'a paranoid type but not a paranoiac', Grierson had been adamant that, at the time Cousins had killed his wife, he had known right from wrong.

The defence having rested, it was left to Mr Justice Croom-Johnson to sum up the case. He instructed the jury that they could return one of three verdicts – not guilty, guilty or guilty but insane. There was, he pointed out, no dispute about the facts of the case, but there was a dispute about the state of Cousins' mind and the onus of proof of mental impairment rested with the defence. There had been nothing in Cousins' mental history prior to the murders to suggest insanity – in fact all that was known about him was that he was apparently a hard-working and respectable man with a kindly disposition.

The judge emphasised the importance of the various items of correspondence written and received by Cousins between 22 May and 8 July. The jury would probably agree that Cousins was an abnormal person, but did what they had heard in court indicate that he was insane? Reminding them that they should only be considering the case that was before them – that of the murder of Mary Ann Cousins – the judge pointed out that all three of the medical witnesses called had identified some degree of mental illness in the defendant. However, there was disagreement between the prosecution and the defence as to the extent of that illness. Were the jury satisfied by the medical witnesses called by the defence, who believed that, at the time of the murder of his wife, Cousins was labouring under a defect of reason that prevented him from knowing the nature and quality of what he was doing?

The jury retired for an hour and a half before returning a verdict of 'Guilty'. Immediately, the clerk of the court asked Cousins if he had anything to say that sentence should not be passed on him. Cousins began to speak, but his voice was so quiet that the judge didn't even realise that he was speaking. He put on his black cap and sentenced Cousins to be executed. Cousins, who showed no sign of emotion at his sentence, was removed from the court, at which the judge discharged the jury and ordered that the case of the murder of Edith Jessie Cable should be marked 'not proceeded with'.

At this point, it was brought to the judge's attention that Cousins had tried to speak but had not been recognised. The judge immediately ordered that Cousins be brought back to court and given the opportunity to speak. Cousins, however, merely wanted to assure the judge that he was confident that he had received a fair trial and that he sincerely regretted causing trouble to the families concerned, particularly his own family. He hoped that they would soon forgive and forget him. 'Edie,' said Cousins, 'was one of the pleasantest women and best women a man could wish to live with and for that reason I am still willing and prepared to die for her only.'

Willing or not, Cousins was not to get his wish. The man who intended to die on 'Winchester Scaffold' was later reprieved, certified insane and ordered to be detained at Broadmoor Asylum.

24

'EITHER YOU DO WHAT I WANT YOU TO DO OR YOU DIE'

Marlborough, 1943

Twenty-two-year-old Muriel Fawden had spent a pleasant evening at the cinema in Marlborough and, as she left, she bumped into a friend, Cynthia June Lay, usually known as June. The two girls both worked at Savernake Hospital, near Marlborough, June as an assistant cook and Muriel as a secretary. At around eight o'clock on 28 September 1943, the women set off to walk back to the hospital together. It was still daylight as they strolled along talking. Suddenly a black American soldier appeared behind them, seemingly out of nowhere, and asked where they were going.

Although the man had startled the girls, Muriel politely replied that they were heading for the hospital and that it wasn't too far away. However, she had no intention of stopping and chatting with the man, so continued on towards the hospital, walking more quickly than before in the hope of leaving the soldier behind.

They had not gone much further when they heard a shout; 'Stand still or I'll shoot.' Muriel and June stopped in their tracks, turning to see the soldier aiming his rifle at them. The terrified girls froze as the soldier rushed up to them, still covering them with his rifle.

He ordered them to get through the hedge into a field at the side of the road. Muriel pointed out that they would be unable to do so, as the hedge was interwoven with barbed wire. The soldier gestured with his rifle, indicating that they should walk back in the direction from which they had come.

As they were marched along at gunpoint, walking backwards to face their attacker, eighteen-year-old June Lay suddenly decided to try and escape. Shouting to Muriel to make a run for it, she made her break for freedom. The soldier raised his rifle and fired twice and June immediately dropped to the ground, mortally wounded. The soldier then aimed his gun at Muriel, firing several times and, as

Marlborough High Street in the 1920s. (Author's collection)

the bullets whistled past her, she realised that her best hope of survival lay in acquiescing to the soldier's demands, whatever they might be. She stopped running and waited for the man to catch up with her.

She was then forced into a field at the side of the road. The soldier stood over her, pointing his gun at her and told her, 'Either you do what I want you to do or you die.' Muriel hesitated for a moment and the soldier said menacingly, 'I am going to count to ten.' Muriel was ordered to remove her white mackintosh coat, which she could not do without first taking off her gloves. Having handed the gloves to the soldier, she dropped her coat on the ground. The soldier then laid down his own greatcoat and subjected the frightened girl to a prolonged rape and sexual assault, which lasted for several hours.

At one point, Muriel could see torchlights and realised that people must be out searching for her. The soldier hurriedly pushed her into some bushes out of sight, ordering her to keep still and quiet and threatening to shoot anyone who came near. Eventually the people with torches went away and Muriel was subjected to a further sexual assault.

Realising that it was now up to her to try and save her own life, Muriel began talking to her captor. She told him that she was a nurse and that she would get into trouble for being out late. She then asked the soldier if he was a Christian, promising to pray for him and to forgive him if he would only let her go. Much to her surprise, the soldier agreed to do just that. Ironically, he asked her if she would be afraid walking by herself and insisted on walking with her to a wicket gate, where Muriel politely bade him 'Goodbye' and set off towards the hospital, all the while expecting a shot in the back. When it didn't come, she broke into a run, but soon found herself helplessly lost among the trees of Savernake Forest.

Meanwhile, two tanker drivers, employed by Bulwark Transport Co., had been returning from their regular run, transporting milk from Wiltshire to London. Driving up Savernake Hill on the main London road, Robert Freeman had seen the body of a young woman lying in the road in a pool of blood. Assuming that there had been a road accident, he stopped his vehicle and sent his colleague,

Savernake Hospital, Marlborough. (Author's collection)

Mr Beasley, to fetch the police while he attended to the girl, who was still alive despite having serious head injuries. Within a few moments, two girls from the Savernake Hospital arrived, quickly followed by an Army cadet who had heard two shots minutes before and had come to investigate.

By the time the police and a doctor reached the scene ten minutes later, the young woman, identified by the two girls from the hospital as June Lay, had died from her injuries. At a later post-mortem examination, conducted by Dr Maurice and Dr Bashall, it was determined that she had been shot twice, once in the head and once in the back and had died as a result of damage caused by the bullet passing through her brain. Her death was the latest in a series of tragedies that had recently befallen her family – her stepmother had died less than a month earlier and, shortly afterwards, her brother was seriously injured at work and, at the time of his sister's death, was still being treated in hospital for a badly crushed foot.

Muriel Fawden was eventually found by PC Bowyer, in a distressed and hysterical state, cowering in undergrowth about 300yds from the place where June had fallen. She was immediately taken to Savernake Hospital, where she was medically examined and put to bed. As a result of her statement to the police, they went directly to a nearby American Army camp where an immediate bed check showed that two men were missing. One was legitimately absent on guard duty, the other – Private Lee A. Davis – was nowhere to be found and his bunk had not been slept in that night.

By now, an American Army cap had been found in undergrowth, a few yards from where June Lay had fallen. It was marked inside 'W 8470' and was found to belong to Private Wheeler from the American camp, who, on the night before the murder, had lent it to Private Davis. As Davis closely matched the description given by Muriel Fawden, he was promptly arrested and charged with rape and murder.

Marlborough Town Hall. (Author's collection)

The investigation was jointly handled by the civilian police from Marlborough and by American Army officers. Having been fully advised of his rights by Major Hugh Foster, Davis agreed to answer questions, the answers to which were subsequently typed. When asked to sign the transcript, Davis then said that he wished to make his own statement, rather than simply answer questions about what had happened. In this statement, Davis admitted attacking the women, but insisted that he had been very drunk at the time, having spent the evening in Marlborough consuming a mixture of beer, wine, Scotch and aspirins. He stated that he had genuinely believed that he was aiming his rifle into the air when he fired at June Lay and that her death had been a tragic accident.

As a serving member of the American forces, Davis faced a court martial rather than a normal murder trial. The proceedings opened on 8 October 1943, but were adjourned indefinitely, until Muriel Fawden had recovered sufficiently from her ordeal to give evidence.

By 26 October, doctors judged her well enough to testify, although it was stressed that she should not be subjected to an intense cross-examination. Described as a 'slim, attractive brunette', Muriel Fawden only faltered briefly in her testimony, when she recounted the events leading to the death of her friend, June Lay.

Lee Davis pleaded 'Not Guilty' to the charges against him and continued to maintain that he thought his rifle had been pointing into the air when he fired towards June. In his statement he admitted to committing a crime, saying that he knew he should be punished for it. Professing to be very sorry for June's death he said, 'All I ask of you all, will you spare my life?' [*sic*]. However, the evidence against him was overwhelming.

Positively identified by Muriel Fawden as the man who had raped her and shot her friend, Davis had been missing from camp without permission at the crucial time and, at a later inspection, had appeared dishevelled and agitated and had mislaid his carbine. Private Wheeler, who shared a bunkbed with Davis, was carrying the carbine that had been officially issued to Davis, but as the rifles normally hung at the end of the beds it was possible for Wheeler and Davis to have accidentally picked up each other's guns. Wheeler's assigned gun was found hidden behind their hut, with a clip of ammunition. Tests showed that it had been recently fired and striations on the bullets fired from it were identical to those on bullets recovered from the body of June Lay. Wheeler's cap, known to have been in Davis's possession and Davis's khaki trousers and his handkerchief were bloodstained. Furthermore, an empty cartridge case was found in his trouser pocket and Muriel Fawden's gloves were discovered in the pocket of his greatcoat.

The outcome of the court martial was that Private Lee A. Davis was sentenced to death by hanging for the wilful murder of Cynthia June Lay. In addition, he was found guilty of the rape of Muriel Fawden, also an offence punishable by death under American military law. His execution took place on 14 December 1943 at Shepton Mallet prison, part of which had been taken over by the American forces for use as a military prison. Escorted into the execution chamber by hangman Albert Pierrepoint, Davis caught sight of the noose and the grim reality of his situation suddenly hit him. 'Oh God, I'm going to die,' he moaned and, within minutes, he became one of the eighteen American soldiers to be executed at Shepton Mallet.

In his autobiography, Albert Pierrepoint condemned the 'American traditions' surrounding such military executions, at which the prisoner's charges were read out to him while he stood on the gallows, after which he was then allowed to make a final statement. Pierrepoint, who prided himself on conducting executions swiftly and humanely, deplored these refinements to the tried and tested British system, as they could extend the time taken to execute a man by up to twenty minutes.

[Note: There is considerable discrepancy in contemporary newspaper accounts of the murder as to the ages of the victims. June Lay is variously described as being seventeen, eighteen and nineteen years old at the time of her death, while Muriel Fawden is said to be either twenty, twenty-one or twenty-two years old.]

25

'SHE MADE CHRIS GO AWAY'

Swindon, 1953

On the night of 2 June 1953 most people in England went to bed tired but happy, having spent the day enthusiastically celebrating the coronation of Her Majesty Queen Elizabeth II, which had taken place that day at Westminster Abbey. Mr and Mrs Court of College Street, Swindon were no exception. They had attended the Sanford Street Coronation Party, held in a nearby church hall and, as well as enjoying a special tea, had each been given a gift of 10s by the organisers.

The gift of money was not unwelcome to the Courts. Mr Court was a chronic invalid who suffered from heart trouble and had only recently been discharged from hospital. In the struggle to make ends meet, the Courts had opened their home to lodgers and, in June 1953, had two men staying at the house, a third lodger having left just days before.

At just before midnight, the peaceful house was disturbed by desperate shouts of 'Murder!' coming from the downstairs hallway. Lodger Arthur Polsue, a commercial traveller from St Albans, had been asleep in bed for about three quarters of an hour when he was awakened by the commotion. When he went to investigate the noise, he found Mr Court in his pyjamas, lying at the foot of the stairs, shouting.

Having made Mr Court as comfortable as he possibly could, Polsue rushed outside to alert the neighbours and summon help. Mr and Mrs Messenger, who lived next door to the Courts, were initially awakened by the disturbance in their neighbour's home and within moments, another neighbour was knocking at their door, asking to use their telephone. While they were waiting for the police and a doctor to arrive, the Messengers went next door and helped Arthur Polsue to get Mr Court into bed.

Meanwhile, Mrs Beatrice Court had been found sitting in a chair in the kitchen, quite obviously dead. On another kitchen chair, on the opposite side of the room, the Court's second lodger, twenty-seven-year-old factory machine operator John Owen Greenway, sat weeping, his head in his hands. Ivor Messenger noticed that Greenway had blood on his right hand and that there was a bloody hatchet lying on the kitchen floor.

The High Street, Swindon, in the 1920s. (Author's collection)

When the police arrived at just after a quarter past midnight, they arrested Greenway and charged him with the murder of Mrs Court. Greenway was by then in a state of near collapse, begging Inspector Young, 'What have I done? Is she dead? Don't let me see her,' as he was taken away to the police station for questioning. He was charged with Mrs Court's murder at 3.30 a.m. 'There is nothing to say,' stated Greenway in response to the charge.

Later that day, however, he did find something to say, giving a statement to the police explaining precisely why he had so viciously attacked and killed his landlady. It happened, he told them, because 'She made Chris go away.'

Greenway had come to lodge at Mr and Mrs Court's home from his native Pontypridd, Wales in April 1953, in the company of a friend, Christopher Percy, whom he had known for six years. The two men shared what was described in the contemporary newspapers as 'a strong affection for each other'. They also, through their own choice, shared a double bed at their lodgings.

On 29 May, Christopher Percy had unexpectedly left Swindon, without first telling Greenway that he was going. He left a note saying, 'Get out of here as soon as you can as it is the worst food we have ever had in our lives. I have gone. God knows where.' In the letter, Percy also promised that he would telephone Greenway's sister and let her know his whereabouts.

Greenway had telephoned his sister, telling her to expect a telephone call from Christopher Percy. Percy had indeed rung a couple of days later and she had passed a message on to her brother when she had next spoken to him. Greenway had rung his sister again from a telephone kiosk on the evening of the murder, but there had been no further message from Percy.

Having returned to his lodgings after making his telephone call, Greenway decided to confront his landlady, knocking at her bedroom door at between 11.30 and 11.45 p.m. In a rage, he had accused Beatrice Court of driving away his friend by serving such terrible food. Mrs Court argued that Percy's departure was not her fault, at which Greenway showed her the letter from his former roommate. An argument

Swindon, 1920s. (Author's collection)

ensued, during which Greenway picked up a hatchet stored in the kitchen and struck Mrs Court several times over the head. When Mr Court tried to intervene, Greenway attacked him too, injuring his hand, although fortunately not too seriously.

Dr George Henderson, a consultant pathologist, conducted a post-mortem examination on Mrs Court's body. He found seven transverse cuts to the back of her neck at the base of her skull, the longest being 3in. Mrs Court's skull – which Henderson noted was slightly thinner than normal – had several fractures, all of which could have been caused by the hatchet. In addition, there were cuts and bruising to the back of the head and the left hand and severe bruising on the left thigh. Dr Henderson confirmed that the cause of sixty-eight-year-old Beatrice Court's death was destruction of parts of the brain by violence, with resultant bleeding.

Twenty-seven-year-old Greenway appeared before magistrates for the first time on 11 June charged with the murder of his landlady. Mr Pooley, the magistrate's clerk, asked him if he was legally represented, to which Greenway replied, 'No, sir.' He was then offered Legal Aid to appoint counsel, and again replied, 'No, sir.'

'Don't you think you should have someone to represent you?' persisted Pooley.

'I don't know,' replied Greenway. He eventually conceded that he would do whatever the court thought best and solicitor Mr J.D. Morrison was appointed to act on his behalf.

Greenway made several more appearances before magistrates, on each occasion wearing the same brown suit and brown checked shirt without a tie. On one occasion, the proceedings were relocated to a private house in Wellington Street in order to hear evidence from Mr Court who was confined to bed there, seriously ill. The magistrates heard evidence from all the key players in the tragedy, including Mr Polsue, Mr and Mrs Messenger, Detective Sergeant Cuss, Inspector Young and other police officers involved in the investigation. (Mr Polsue brought a moment of light relief to the proceedings – asked by the prosecution counsel about the quality of food at the lodgings, he screwed up his face and admitted that 'It was appalling'.) They also heard from the alleged reason behind the murder, Christopher Percy.

Percy told the court that the food at the lodgings was 'very, very poor'. He had left Swindon partly because he couldn't stomach the food and partly because he needed to sort out his domestic affairs in South Wales. Percy stated that he had not told Greenway about his domestic affairs.

His evidence was followed by that of Mrs Margaret Ritschel, Greenway's sister. She described her last telephone call with her brother on the night of the murder. John had been heartbroken that Christopher had left Swindon, telling his sister that, if Percy did not come back, he would commit suicide. A letter was read out in court by Detective Sergeant Cuss, which Greenway had subsequently written to his sister. In it Greenway wrote, 'I have murdered Mrs Court, the landlady ... I don't think I got any chance. I killed her.' [sic]. According to Cuss, the actual letter had not been forwarded to Margaret Ritschel as his senior officers had considered the contents too crude for her eyes.

John Owen Greenway was eventually committed for trial at the next Wiltshire Assizes and the proceedings opened on 2 October before Mr Justice Parker. When the charge was read out to him at the start of the trial he immediately pleaded 'Guilty' to the murder of Beatrice Ann Court on 2 June.

In spite of advice from his defence counsel, Greenway steadfastly refused to amend his plea to the more customary one of 'Not Guilty'. The judge called the defence counsel to the bench for a conference. The senior defence counsel, Mr A.C. Munro Kerr, explained that he had failed to persuade Greenway to amend his plea, as had his colleague, Mr Inskip, the instructing solicitors and two doctors.

Had the plea been 'Not Guilty', Munro Kerr told the judge, the defence would have questioned Greenway's state of mind at the time of the alleged murder. Two doctors had examined him, with a view to demonstrating that he was not responsible at the time when the act was committed. Munro Kerr told the judge that he now found himself in an awkward position since he was not, at that time, able to determine whether or not his client was fit to plead. At the same time, he was not in a position to state that his client did not understand the effect of the plea he had now made.

All he could say was that he and others had explained the situation to Greenway to the best of their ability and that the accused seemed to be totally logical in his decision. Greenway just wanted to die, which was why he was insisting on pleading 'Guilty'.

Finally, after all efforts to persuade him had failed, Mr Justice Parker himself addressed the prisoner.

'Do you appreciate what you are doing?' he asked Greenway.

'Yes,' was Greenway's reply.

'Do you realise there can only be one result to such a plea?'

'Yes,' said Greenway again.

'Is that your final decision?'

'Yes.'

'Then there is only one sentence which this court can pass upon you,' concluded the judge, reaching for the black cap.

John Owen Greenway, the man who wanted to die, got his wish on 20 October 1953. He was hanged at Horfield Prison, Bristol, by Albert Pierrepoint, assisted by Harry Allen.

26

'EVERYONE SAID SHE WAS TOO PERFECT TO LIVE'

Salisbury, 1953

Twenty-eight-year-old Norman Shilton, a postman, was slowly dying from cancer. He had been seriously ill for more than two years and, by August 1953, it was obvious that he had only a very short time left to live. Only then did Bessie, his devoted wife, ask her mother-in-law, Frances Shilton, to sleep at the house in Queens Road, Salisbury.

On 16 August, Frances left the house at twenty-past eleven in the morning for a brief visit to her own home in Clarendon Road, arranging to return at three o'clock when she promised to take her granddaughter out 'if daddy was still all right'. Bessie assured her that she would telephone her immediately should anything happen to Norman and Frances had no reason to doubt her – after all, Bessie had always been the perfect wife to her son, keeping the house spotless and caring for him devotedly throughout his long illness, refusing to allow him to be taken into hospital.

When she returned at three o'clock, Frances was concerned to find the front door of the house locked against her. She knocked and shouted for several minutes, but there was no answer, so she went through a neighbour's home to get to the back door. That too was locked and, looking through the window into the dining room, where a downstairs bed had been made up for Norman, Frances saw that the bed was empty.

Mrs Shilton turned to the neighbours, Mr and Mrs Pearce, for help and Richard Pearce managed to ease up the sash window in the dining room and climb through it. As he scrambled over Norman's bed, he found his body lying on the floor at the side of it.

A strong smell of gas pervaded the house and Mr Pearce hurried to the kitchen to try and find the source. There, lying on an eiderdown on the kitchen floor, he found Bessie Shilton and her daughter, Linda Bessie, who was two years and

Salisbury High Street and Poultry Cross, 1950s. (Author's collection)

eleven months old. On the kitchen table stood two bottles, one containing Norman Shilton's sleeping tablets, the other junior aspirins. Both mother and daughter appeared dead.

A doctor was immediately called and Linda was taken out into the garden. Dr Clive Sheen attempted artificial respiration and also injected the child, but it was too late. Meanwhile, Bessie Smith, who was alive but deeply unconscious, was rushed to the Salisbury Infirmary. It took two days before she had recovered sufficiently to be told that her daughter was dead.

A post-mortem examination on little Linda confirmed that she had died as a result of carbon monoxide poisoning. She had had a cold and traces of junior aspirin were found in her body, although that had not contributed to her death. That Bessie had intended to kill Linda and herself was blatantly obvious, since she had left two suicide notes, one addressed to 'My own dear Mum and Dad' and the other to Norman's parents.

The letter to her own parents read:

My own dearest Mum and Dad,

Well my dears, I am writing this letter to you with a broken heart for Norman has passed on and now I have nothing left to live for. Don't think I don't love you dearly though. Believe me my dears, I do, oh I do. But my love for Norman was even stronger as ours has been such a perfect partnership and because our love and contentment for each other was so perfect it seems it was too good for us to share for more than four years. For now the light of my life has been taken from me so Linda and I are going to join her beloved Daddy in the world beyond.

Detective Sergeant Thomas Shales charged Bessie Shilton with her daughter's murder while she was still in hospital and, on her discharge she was immediately taken before a special sitting of magistrates at the Guildhall in Salisbury. She was to make four appearances in magistrate's court in all and, between hearings, was remanded in Holloway Prison.

Much was made at the court hearings of the closeness between Bessie and Norman Shilton. According to Norman's mother, even before his illness, her son and his wife had been a devoted couple who shunned visitors, being perfectly content with each other's company and that of their daughter. Not only that, but Bessie was also an exceptionally good mother to Linda and absolutely worshipped her daughter. Frances Shilton told the magistrate's court that the idea of her daughter-in-law killing her granddaughter would be the very last thing she expected.

The district nurse and doctor who had attended Norman throughout his illness were called to give evidence. Dr Sheen, who had tried so hard to resuscitate Linda, had been the Shilton's regular GP. Dr Sheen spoke of the remarkable courage that Bessie had shown throughout her husband's illness. He had visited Norman on the morning of his death, at which time Bessie seemed calm and composed and resigned to the fact that her beloved husband was all too rapidly nearing the end of his life. He too had had no inkling that Bessie might attempt suicide and take her daughter's life as well.

Mrs Olive Norris, the district nurse, had also visited the Shilton's home at about twenty past ten on the morning of Norman's death, a Sunday. Over the course of Norman's illness and her daily calls at the house to attend him, she had come to know the family well. She too testified that Bessie had been her normal self that day and, although she had not seen Linda on that visit, she had been told that the child was upstairs with a slight cold. Mrs Norris told the court of the courage with which both Norman and Bessie had faced his terminal illness. It had been suggested many times that Norman should go into hospital, but neither he nor Bessie would even entertain the idea. Yet while the couple insisted that they just wanted to be together for however long they had left, the mammoth task of nursing her husband day and night, coupled with looking after her home and a young child had put an enormous strain on Bessie, particularly since Norman was in great pain for the months prior to his death.

One of the final witnesses called before the magistrates was WPC Phyllis Thomas, who had been assigned to guard Bessie Shilton at Salisbury Infirmary. She testified that Bessie had told her that Linda 'cried in my arms because her daddy was dead. I could not bear it. I didn't mean to kill her. She was perfect. Everyone said she was too perfect to live – and I loved her so much. She was such a comfort to me in all the trouble I had.'

Twenty-five-year-old Bessie Shilton sat in court, crying quietly as the evidence against her unfolded. An attractive, dark-haired young woman, dressed in a grey coat over a flower-patterned summer dress, she remained calm, if visibly upset. When the chief magistrate informed her that she was to be committed to stand trial at the next Wiltshire Assizes for the murder of her daughter, she smiled faintly at him and whispered, 'Yes, sir. Thank you.'

The trial at Devizes was presided over by Mr Justice Parker and Bessie Shilton pleaded 'Not Guilty' to the murder of her daughter, Linda Bessie. John Stephenson defended Mrs Shilton and Mr H.J. Phillimore QC prosecuted.

Most of the witnesses from the magistrate's court testified at the assizes and, from the beginning, it seemed very much as though the emphasis of the proceedings were on Bessie Shilton's mental state at the time of the murder.

Frances Shilton again championed her daughter-in-law, telling the court that there was no better housewife in the world than Bessie. According to Mrs Shilton, Bessie kept her house and her daughter beautifully clean and had never once been heard to complain about her circumstances. Unwilling to be apart from Norman for even a minute, she had slept on two chairs in his bedroom night after night. Watching her adored husband in constant pain and slowly dying had been a terrible strain on her.

Dr Sheen and Nurse Norris echoed Mrs Shilton in describing the effects of Norman's illness on Bessie Shilton, both saying that, towards the end, the signs of her extreme strain were clearly visible.

The defence called the only new witness, Dr Thomas Christie, the principal medical officer at Holloway Prison. Christie had been caring for Bessie Shilton since her arrival at Holloway on 20 August and described her as both severely depressed and clearly suffering from a disease of the mind. Had he been Mrs Shilton's private physician, he added, he would have unhesitatingly arranged for her immediate admission to a mental hospital for observation.

Christie stated that she had become almost obsessive in caring for her husband, wanting to be at his side for twenty-four hours a day just in case he needed her. He also pointed out that Bessie was afraid that Norman's illness may be hereditary and so might be visited on her little girl. This left Bessie under such a tremendous pressure that, when she killed Linda, she had a severe defect of reason that would have left her totally incapable of knowing that what she was doing was wrong. On the contrary, what she was doing in trying to join Norman with her daughter would have seemed absolutely the right thing to do.

Uppermost in Bessie Shilton's mind was the loss of her soul mate and the fact that Linda had been so distraught at the death of her daddy. It was only too easy to see that, for Bessie, the only option was that the closely-knit family should stay together and that her only motive for killing her daughter and attempting to kill herself was that she and her daughter should be as a family with Norman again, wherever he might be.

Dr Christie finished by telling the court that Bessie had made a steady improvement since her admission to prison. What he described as 'the severe phase' had now passed, although he could not rule out the possibility of a recurrence. At present, he could not regard her as certifiably insane, although he believed that she most probably was at the time of the murder.

It was left to the counsels for the prosecution and defence to make their closing arguments and even Phillimore for the prosecution seemed largely sympathetic towards Bessie. Calling the circumstances of the case tragic and pitiful in the extreme, he nevertheless reminded the jury that it was their duty to give a verdict in accordance with the law.

After a three-and-a-half-hour trial, the jury of nine men and three women needed only five minutes to decide on their verdict, finding Bessie Ruth Irene Shilton 'Guilty but insane'. Mr Justice Parker ordered that she be detained as a patient at Broadmoor Hospital until Her Majesty's pleasure be made known.

Broadmoor Asylum, 1906. (Author's collection)

Bessie had shown little emotion throughout the trial and while she undoubtedly deeply regretted killing her only daughter, it is probably fair to say that her deepest regret was having survived her attempted suicide.

BIBLIOGRAPHY & REFERENCES

BOOKS

Eddleston, John J., *The Encyclopaedia of Executions*, London, John Blake, 2004
Evans, Roger, *Wiltshire Tales of Mystery and Murder*, Newbury, Countryside Books, 2005
Pierrepoint, Albert, *Executioner Pierrepoint*, Kent, Hodder and Stoughton, 1980

ARTICLES

Taylor, Kay, 'Murder at Brookside Cottage: a Dark Deed in North Wiltshire', *Wiltshire Archaeological & Natural History Magazine*, Vol. 04, 2001, pp 47-55

NEWSPAPERS

Bath Herald
Salisbury and Wiltshire Journal
Swindon Evening Advertiser
The Times

Certain websites have also been consulted in the compilation of this book, but since they have a habit of disappearing, to avoid frustration, they have not been cited.

INDEX

Abrahams, Richard 51
Adams, Florence 64–67
Adye, Mr W. 20
Alderbury 103
Alexander, Mr 49
Allen, Harry 118
Amesbury 84, 106
Asher, John 18
Ashley 33–34
Asser (Hasser), Verney 88–92
Atkins, John 21
Avory, Mr Justice 91–92

Bailey, Hannah 41
Bailey, PC Alfred 55–56
Baker, Nicholas 21–24
Baker, Sarah 21–24
Baldwin, Superintendent 61
Barbour, Dr R.F. 108
Bashall, Dr 112
Bath, PC Thomas 35
Bathe, William 9–13
Baxter, Robert 96
Bear Inn, The 44–45
Beasley. Mr 112
Beaufort, Duke of 21
Belcher, Edward 13
Bell Inn, The 11
Bench, George and Samuel 47
Bentham 10
Berry, James 58, 62
Berwick St John 47
Best, Mr Justice 12
Bignell, William Grover 93–96
Billington, James 67, 71
Billington, John 71
Billington, Thomas 71
Billington, William 71
Bingham, Mr 20
Bishop, William 45
Blake, Phoebe 26–28
Blanchett, Mr 11
Bowyer, PC 112

Box 33–36
Bradford on Avon 7–8, 19, 53, 63, 84
Brain, Mrs 96
Brakeworth, PC John 23–24
Bratton 40
Britton, Henry 39
Broadmoor Asylum 109, 122
Brown, James 43–45
Brown, Mrs 20
Brown, Robert 19–21
Buchanan Smith, Mr S 78
Buckland (Buckley) Edward 14–18
Bull, Inspector 51
Burbage 72–76
Burgess, PC James 39–42
Burt, Mr 49
Buscombe, James 22–24
Bush, John 19–21
Butt, Thomas 51

Casberd, Mr 12–13
Cable, Edith Jessie 103–109
Calcraft, William 49
Callaway, Ann 41
Cannings, James 85
Carter, Mrs 80
Charles, Mr Justice 67
Chitty, George 49
Christian Malford 17
Christie, Dr Thomas 122
Churchill, Winston 76
Clark, James 20
Cockle, Elizabeth 37– 41
Coleman, Mr 15
Coleman, Stephen 50–52
Coleridge, Mr Justice / Lord Chief Justice 36,
    51–52, 74
Cook, Sergeant 47–48
Cornewall-Lewis, Sir G. 48
Corsley 65
Cottle, Elizabeth 15–18
Court, Beatrice 115–118
Court, Mr 115–118

Cousins, Kathleen 104–106
Cousins, Mary Ann 103–108
Cousins, William Hugh 103–109
Cousins, William Hugh junior 106
Cowrie, Dr 60
Cox, Henry 12
Cozens, Sophia 13
Cresswell, Mr Justice 39–42
Cricklade 9–12
Crook, PC 96
Croom-Johnson, Mr Justice 106–108
Crouch, Sgt William 84–87
Cuss, Det. Sergeant 117–118

Dale, Mr H. 106
Dampier, Mr 27
Daniel, PC John 20
Darling, Mr Justice 81–82
Davis, Lee A 112–114
Devizes 24, 35, 39, 42, 49, 50–52, 56–58, 59–63,
    64, 67, 71, 79–81, 91,121
Dew, Chief Inspector 78
Dickens, James 28
Dine, John 29–30
Dix, Sophia 29–21
Dolamore, Dr W.H. 74
Drury, Mrs 93–96
Durkin, Joseph Harold 88–92
Durrington 103–109

Eagles, Thomas 12
Edwards, Mr 36
Edwards, Mr A.L. 85–86
Elkins, Inspector 74
Ellery, PC Richard 17
Ellis, John 92
Elms Cross 53
Emmanuel, Mr S.H. 74, 91–92
Enford 84–87
Erle, Mr Justice 45

Farquhar, Dr 72–75
Fawden, Muriel 110–114
Ferris, Thomas 18
Fiddler, Samuel 104
Fidler, William 72
Fisherton Anger 8, 17, 21, 24
Flowers, Ann 14–17
Foot, Mr 46
Foote, Mr J.A. 69–70, 79–81, 91
Foster, Major Hugh 113
Fox Inn, The 94
Freeman, Robert 111–112

Gale, James 35
Gane, William 30–31
Gay (Gray), Samuel 97–102
Gerrish, Charles 50–52
Gibbs, Mr J.H. 39
Giles, Charles 25–28

Goddard, Mr Rayner 74–75, 79–82
Golding, William 80–82
Goldstone, Mr 35
Green, Mr 47
Greenway, John Owen 115–118
Greenwood, William 17
Grierson, Dr Hugh 108
Griffith, Mr 29
Grimes, Phoebe 9–13
Grove Inn, The 33
Groves, Mr Justice 56–58
Guirdham, Dr Arthur 107–108
Gurd, John (aka Hamilton, Louis) 64–67

Habgood, John 9–13
Haddow, Mr 39
Hall, Dr Walter 99
Hampton, Caleb 59–63
Hampton, Edward 59–63
Harding, William 19–20
Harris, Jane 41
Harris, Mr 65
Harris, Superintendent 47–48
Harrison, Revd 13
Haskell, Edwin Richard 77–83
Haskell, Flora Fanny 77–83
Haskell, Miss 81–82
Hassall, Henry 50–52
Hawke, Mr E.A 95
Hayward, Dr Joseph 15
Hayward, Richard 50–52
Hemmerde, Mr KC 100–101
Henderson, Dr George 117
Henderson, Mr Scott 106
Herapath, William 42, 49
Hicks, William 12
Highmore, Dr 54–57
Highworth 29–32
Hillier, Mr 60
Hillier, Mrs 73–75
Hobbs, Samuel 54–56
Hodges, Mr 45
Holloway Prison 121–122
Holroyd, Mr Justice 17
Holt, Reginald 95–96
Horfield Prison 118
Horton, Caroline 55–56
Horton, Edward 53–58
Horton, John 53–58
Horton, John junior 53–57
Hughes, Mr M. 106
Hulse, Lady 78
Hussey Walsh, Mr 61–62
Hythe 47–48

Inskip, Mr 118

Jeffreys, John 47
Jones, Eliza 29–32
Joyce, Jane 41

Kempe, Dr 80
Kibblewhite, James 13

Lacey, Mr 68
Lacock 21–24
Langley Fitzurze 15
Langley, PC 66
Lawes, Mr Thornton 69
Lay, Cynthia June 110–114
Lee, Richard 19–21
Legg, Margaret 93–96
Lemon, Mr A.B.106–107
Leviathan 36
'Lincoln, John' 99–102
Lindsey (Tarrant), Charlotte 53–58
Little, Ann 33–36
Little, George 33
Little, Grenada 33
Little, Isaac 33 –35
Little, James 33
Little, James and Ann 33
Little, Thomas 33–35
Littledale, Mr Justice 31–32
Littleton Drew 19–21
Llewellyn, Captain 86
Longleat Park 66
Long Newnton 93–96
Lopes Arms, The 39–40
Lopes, Mr 39, 51–52, 56, 61,
Lower Westbrook 53–58

MacKay, Patrick 18
Mackey, Charlotte 40–41
Maitland 36
Manzano, Serafin 48–49
Marlborough 74, 110–114
Martin, Richard 47
Marwood, William 52
Mathews, Mr Charles 56–58
Maurice, Dr Oliver 74, 112
Mayell, John 44–45
Mead, John 55
Mead, Prudence 40
Melksham 64–67
Mereweather, Mr Sergeant 20–21, 36
Merritt, Sergeant 94–96
Messenger, Mr and Mrs 115–117
Millard, Sarah 41
Milne, Corporal 88–92
Mold, Mr 80
Molden, Enos 66–67
Moon, Egbert 27
Morrison, Mr J.D. 117
Mumford, Alfred 40–42
Munro-Kerr, Mr A.C 118
Murch, Mr 56

Napper, Daniel 43–45
Napper, Dennis 43–45
Napper, James 43–45

Napper, Mary Ann 43–45
Nash, Mary Ann 72–76
Nash, Stanley George 72–75
Neighbour, Dr 106
Netheravon 84
Newman, Ann 37
Newman, Humphrey 39–42
Noble, Alfred 80–82
Noble, Percy 77–81
Norris, Olive 121
Nugent, James 92
Nunn, George 27

O'Brien cousins 104
Ockwell, Henry 12
Ockwell, Thomas 12

Packer, Henry 12
Palmer, Edward Richard 68–71
Palmer, Sir Walter and Lady 78
Park, Mr Justice 20–21, 24, 27–28
Parker, Mr Justice 118, 121–122
Parkhurst Prison 101
Parr, Mr T.H. 79, 91
Parsons, Caroline 47
Parsons, Mrs 46
Pearce, Judith 14–18
Pearce, Mr and Mrs 119
Pearce, William 44–45
Peer, Wilfred 94–96
Pepper, Mr / Professor 74, 80–82
Percy, Christopher 115–118
Perrett, Superintendent 66–67
Phillimore, Mr H.J. QC 121–122
Pierce, PC 105
Pierrepoint, Albert 114, 118
Pierrepoint, Thomas 96, 102
Pike, Amelia 85
Pike, PC Ernest 84–87
Pirie, Captain 68
Pizer, PC Joseph 27
Pollock, Baron 61
Polsue, Arthur 115–117
Pooley, Mr 117
Powell, Daniel 15
Preedy, Mr 54
Price, John 15
Purnell (Purcell) Benjamin 59–63
Purnell (Purcell) Emily 59–63
Purton 9
Purton Stoke 9–13

Radcliffe, Mr F.R.Y. 61–62, 74
Rawlings, Thomas 80–82
Richards, Edward Charles Ingram 97–102
Richards, Henry 64–67
Richardson, Mark 78
Ridley, Mr Justice 79–81
Ritschel, Margaret 118
Roberts, Mr G.D. 95

Roberts, William Fletcher 20
Roche, Mr Justice 95–96, 101
Rodway, Mary 9
Rodway, Stephen 9–13
Rose, Mary Ann 26–27
Rowe, Dr 80

Salisbury 7, 17, 28, 32, 35, 45, 74, 77–83, 104, 119–122
Salisbury Football Club 78
Savernake Hospital 110–114
Scaley, Thomas 30–31
Schuster, Mr 79
Scott, Superintendent 90
Sedgwick, Dr Richard 95
Selman, PC 61
Seton, Mr 69
Seymour, Ann 13
Shales, Det. Sergeant Thomas 121
Sharland, George 39
Shaw, Captain Walter MP 101
Sheen, Dr Clive 120–121
Shepton Mallet Prison 92, 96, 102, 114
Sherwood, Thomas 19–21
Shilton, Bessie 119–123
Shilton, Frances 119–122
Shilton Linda Bessie 119–122
Shilton, Norman 119–122
Ship Inn, The 68–71
Shittle, Dr Richard 46
Shrewton 66
Simpkins, William 10
Skelhorn, Mr J. 106
Slade, Mr 39
Slade, PC 85–87
Smith, Francis 34
Smith, Isaac 33–36
Smith, James 33
Smith, Philip 37–42
Smith, Rebecca 37–42
Spencer, Edward 22–24
Stagg, Emma 73–74
Stagg, Ephraim 73–74
Stagg, Mary Jane 72–73
Stapleton, Mr 44–45
Stephenson, John 121–122
Steer, Gertrude 78
Steer, Walter 77–79
Stewart, Ian Ronald Maxwell 99–102
Stingimore, Alice 47
Stokes, William 53
Stone, Harriet 25–28
Stourton, Walter 97–99
Stracey, James 47
Sutton Benger 14–18
Sutton Veny 88–92
Swan, The 34
Sweetman, Emily 80
Swindon 68–71, 84, 93, 115–118
Swinford, Esther 68–71
Sylvester, Mr F.A.P. 61, 86

Talbot, Mr Justice 100–101
Taylor, Mr 40–41
Tennant, Lady 78
Tetbury 94–95
Thomas, WPC Phyllis 121
Thompson, Nathaniel 21
Thompson, Thomas 20–21
Thornton Lawes, Mr 69
Three Horse Shoes, The 53–56
Tollard Royal 46–49
Trebitsch–Lincoln, Ignatius 101
Trebitsch–Lincoln, Ignatius junior (see 'John Lincoln')
Trebitsch–Lincoln, Julius 100–101
Trowbridge 43–45, 97–102
Trowbridge, Anastasia 46–49
Trowbridge, George 46–48
Tuck, Sarah 22–24
Tuck, Thomas 22–24
Tucker, Ann 7–8
Tucker, Samuel 7–8
Tye, Charlotte 35

Underwood, Superintendent Alf 99
Upavon 85

Vickery, John 10–13

Wadley, John 26–28
Wadley, Mary 27–28
Walter, Richard 20
Wansbrough, Mr 101
Warminster 25–28, 66
Watkins, Edward 10–12
Watkins, Robert 9–13
Waylen, Mr 50–52
Wells, Nathaniel 10
Wells, William 9–13
Westbury 37–42
Wheeler, Private 112–114
White Hart Inn (Burbage) The 72
White Hart Inn (Corsley), The 65
White Hart Inn (Cricklade), The 11
Whiteparish 27
Wilkes, Dr 80
Wills, Mr Justice 69–71
Witmarsh, Mr W.B. 35
Wootton Bassett 9–10
Wootton under Edge 94–96
Wright, Dr Michael 99
Wyatt, John Stanley 78–79
Wynn, Henry 29–32

Young, Inspector 116–117

Zebedee, PC 104–106
Zededee, Superintendent 95